THE OTHER VOICE

In 2005, it seemed to me that most of America felt buyer's remorse about the 2004 election. An underperforming president had been re-elected – just barely so, even with the overwhelming benefit of incumbency, and of calling himself a war president. The cost of the Iraq invasion was a heavy stone around the neck of America. Our great country was being ripped in two by forces bent on creating division and anger as a means of mobilizing their voter base.

For the next two years, I wrote for a local newspaper column called "Other Voices." I find that the writings are surprisingly relevant years later. Voters are again crying buyer remorse, this time about the 2010 elections. The stone around our necks has pulled us down into the depths of the Great Recession. That stone will keep our children and their children underwater for decades. That stone threatens ultimately to drown America.

And the country is being further torn by new forces interested primarily in making media money by keeping us angry, not just at the state of America in general, but at each other.

The goal in writing this book was to gather my writings from the mid-2000s in order to remind ourselves why we so badly wanted change and why we had such great hope. By 2004, we were frustrated and angry, and somehow allowed the president to be re-elected, or the election to be stolen without an argument. Shortly thereafter we understood the magnitude of our blunder, but it was too late. We had to wait until 2006, and 2008, to do something about it. The wave of Obamic change inspired us and took us into the next decade, but we should have been mature and insightful enough to understand that a wave of change would not be enough to force the system itself to change. That would take time, and a large segment of independent voters was not patient enough to wait. In 2010, we voted back into office the very folks who had screwed up the system in the first place.

When I wrote the "Other Voices" columns that appeared in the *Chelsea Standard* between 2005 and 2008, I tried very hard to maintain objectivity. Of course, doing so is impossible by definition. Neutrality was also impossible, considering that my political views, my sentiments, and my philosophy are all left of center, and my opinions are very strong. But I always tried to put in enough thought and consideration of all viewpoints that I had at least a fighting chance of being honestly fair and balanced.

Few of us pick the liberal or the conservative side every time, regardless of the issue or the argument. Those who do so are doing a disservice to America and to themselves. Sadly, they are often the loudest and they control the political debate, rendering powerless those who are more rational and open-minded.

Sometime around 2008, Michelle Rogers, editor of the *Chelsea Standard*, was promoted (and rightly so) within the Heritage organization and replaced by a local editor who did speak loudly, control the political debate, and do his best to undermine my work. He wrote rebuttals to my op-eds, getting the last word every time. *How dare he use his biased voice to silence my biased voice?*

Just kidding there, but in the end, he won the battle and accomplished his apparent aim and/or that of the conservative management of the organization. I dug some forty-year-old cameras out of the attic, bought some black and white film, and switched gears from writing to photography. He went on to the sports beat.

I was inspired to start writing again in 2011 after reading a letter in the local *Sun Times News* newspaper. The logic and passion seemed born of many hours sitting on the sofa staring at Fox News, and thus so one-dimensionally misleading that I could not stop myself from responding. To my slight regret, I took a side that appeared just as radical, when in fact my intent was to use dry humor and sarcasm to make readers think. I failed. The voice I used overshadowed my message. I ignored the advice of my friends who told me that my letter was not in keeping with my reputation, with the voice that people had come to trust.

I've included as much of the entire exchange as I could in a special section midway through this book. My letter is an example of what not to do when writing an op-ed or letter to the editor of your local newspaper. Not that editors don't love a good weeks-long battle on the letters page kicked off by a strongly-worded letter. It sells papers, I suppose. But at this moment in history, what we need more than someone being right and someone being wrong is everyone working together.

Here are some of the issues that have bothered me, issues we can come together and do something about:

- Government Spending, School Budgets, and Potholes
- Invading, Rebuilding, and the So-Called Threat of Terrorism
- The Wealth Gap, and Voting Against Our Own Interests
- The Oil Crisis, the Sun, Wind, Birds, and Nuclear Reactors
- Calculated Divisiveness, Rupert Murdoch, and Fairness and Balance
- Special Interests, Influence in Government, and Corporations as People

My "Other Voices" columns touched on these and other topics, many of them local. My goal with this book is to bring them all together under an umbrella of unity, of working together.

Divided we fall, and it has been a divided society that has hurled the pendulum back and forth, in wide swings, in the last four elections. Our legislators have in turn chewed us up and passed us across the aisle to the next party with each swing.

We live in a society that's in shambles, where anger runs high, where hope runs low, and where there seems to be no relief in sight. As voters, as citizens, and as patriots, we can change that.

I hope that after reading this book, and recognizing the similarities between the state of the union in 2011 and the state of the union in 2005, you'll consider voting in 2012, and voting for the right kind of change in Congress.

– Roy

AUTHOR'S NOTE

I've decided to leave the articles in roughly chronological order. I feel grouping them some other way, such as by subject, would be arbitrary.

Also, the dates in the chapter headings reflect the dates I submitted (or saved!) the writings. Sometimes they appeared two days later, in the Wednesday printing of the paper, sometimes they showed up a week later, and sometimes they disappeared into the ether. The curious, bored, and/or obsessive/compulsive reader is welcome to sift through Chelsea Standard archives and identify the actual publication dates.

Finally, being the author, I have enjoyed the privilege of being able to make slight edits or corrections to my original words; to write bridge pieces where I thought they would help; and to insert some of my favorite photographs, which otherwise would probably only be seen by friends, contacts, and random lurkers on my Flickr account. Many of them were taken with vintage, low-fidelity cameras like my original Diana, Brownie Hawkeye, or FujiPet. The photos are not generally related to their adjacent chapters.

I would like to thank my writing pals, George, Michael, and Dave, who spent much time reading these words when they were first written, and again when they were collected here, edited, and bridged together with glue. Their suggestions for improvement have always been on the mark and invaluable.

Thanks to my wife and family for their faith, support, and patience.

And I would like to express my gratitude to my good friend Elsie, who provided the motivation and inspiration, and literally made this book happen. Thank you, El.

T his journey began with a simple letter to the editor in 2005. I enjoyed my local newspaper, the *Chelsea Standard*, and every week I would read it front to back. The commentary pages were interesting, the topics local and relevant, the voices varied. Only one thing was out of place – the weekly editorial by Lansing veteran Tim Skubick. I respected neither his tone nor his talent, but my opinion is worth nothing more than yours, or his, or the editor's, or the reader's.

There was a key reason to criticize the inclusion of Skubick's column in our local paper: the topics were all Lansing focused. In each, he grumbled about some state-level political issue of which most people were not even aware. Nowhere else in the paper was Michigan political news covered, so there was no perspective or context for that one column. It stood out like bird dropping on a dress shirt.

And so, my first letter to the editor of the *Chelsea Standard*.

CHAPTER 1

On Skubick – June 4, 2005

Dear Editor:

His name is Skubick, and he's usually featured in the "Other Voices" column on the "Commentary" page. He is advertised as an objective "veteran observer of Lansing politics."

In fact, if you read his column, he's more than that. He has a clear conservative bias that he sneaks insidiously into his writing. He's that kind of journalist who's not willing to make his point with vigor, provide solid for support it, and make a stand; instead he couches his opinions in the safe and easy "some people are saying this or that" cushion.

For example, in the June 2 issue, he writes about some key elected officials attending a rally for education. In one paragraph, he says, "If they don't show up, somebody will not only question their commitment to education, but they might be called hypocrites."

Come on, Mr. Skubick, are you the one who's questioning their commitment to education? As an objective, veteran political observer, shouldn't you be able to give us, with some authority and objectivity, an accurate assessment of that commitment? Are you the one who's calling them hypocrites? If not, then who is that "somebody?"

There are other choices for "Other Voices," and it would be better to pick someone who's trying to inform objectively; who is discussing a pertinent, current, local issue; or who is working to unite people politically, not continuing to divide them with shadowy jabs at the other side.

I don't see where Skubick's column does anyone a service. It's not news; it's not clear political commentary (at least Rush or Bill or Rachel would be); and it does not serve up any solutions or unifying causes. It doesn't have a place in the Heritage Newspapers, and should be abandoned.

    Thanks.
    Sincerely,
    Roy Schmidt, Chelsea

> To Ryan Maree —
>
> Hope you enjoy the book - lots of passion, hard work, & time (way too many months dragging my feet!) went into this, but it was a fun process. Enjoy!
>
> Roy Schmidt
> 10/27/12

Shortly after I sent my Skubick letter, I received an email from *Chelsea Standard* editor Michele Rogers. She had just embarked on a coffeehouse tour called Meet the Editor, and she invited me to come down to Pierce's Pastries in Chelsea.

We had a nice chat, and I somehow convinced her that I could write and would not embarrass myself or the newspaper if she would let me do some work. As a starting point, she asked, would I be willing to submit an op-ed ("opposite the editorial page" – the writings on the editorial page itself are written by the editor and newspaper staff) for what she called the "Other Voices" column?

I pedaled my bike home, pushed my contracting work aside, pulled up a blank Word doc, and came face to face with the realization that I needed an idea before I could start.

Within a week I had one. A tragic event had happened in town a few months before, and now people came together in response, people of all social levels, all backgrounds, all political leanings. I was impressed. And along with my compassion for the young man who was hurt, I also felt a yearning for this kind of unity to spread over a wider range of America.

My first official "Other Voices" column was published in May of 2005 in the *Chelsea Standard*. Many thanks to Michelle Rogers who encouraged me and published my writing.

This piece still stands to remind us how much we have in common and how unified we are, in spite of the way we are constantly being told that we are a divided populace.

CHAPTER 2

Unity – May 5, 2005

Don't let anyone tell you we're a divided people. We're not.

In August of 2004, Brian Livengood was limbing trees for a friend of the family. He was electrocuted and suffered brain damage. Last Saturday, about 700 people united to stage and attend a benefit for the Livengoods. They raised more than $25,000 to support Brian in his fight to recover.

My family and the Livengoods attend the same church. I like the mix of people there, all friendly. Sure, a handful are strict conservatives who, for example, opposed the Martin Luther King celebration. Some are open-minded liberals who helped usher in our first-ever woman pastor. The majority are plain old down-to-earth Americans, with common values to match. Common values that match.

In the pews of my church, I can point out the Republicans I know, the Democrats too. But that leaves most of the congregation undeclared as far as I know. Outside in the parking lot, you see a few W-04 stickers, a few lingering Kerry/Edwards, a couple NRA, some StopTheNRA.org, some pro-choice, some pro-life. But most bumpers in the lot are clean. Most people aren't political enough to flaunt a bumper sticker.

Every day for the last six years, Big News would have you believe that we are a country divided. Red or Blue. Liberal or Conservative. Pro-Life or Pro-Choice. Fascist or Socialist. Either, but never neither.

But look around you – at your congregation, your office, your school, your neighborhood, your extended family. We're not all that different. We're certainly not divided. The tie-dyed, body-pierced peacenik represents a miniscule portion of the Left. Don't let anyone tell you all liberals are like that. The rigid, anti-choice fanatic represents a small percentage of the Right. Don't let anyone tell you all conservatives are like that.

"If you aren't one of us, you're one of them" is bunk. You don't have to choose a side.

"Us against them" has been spun into "them against us." "They" are attacking freedom; "they" are attacking marriage; "they" are attacking our rights; "they" are staging a war on Christmas. Who are "they" anyway? Either "all you conservatives," or "all you liberals."

But it's not, and we all know it. It's a smoke screen. Misdirection. Manipulation.

You and I, we're not they. We are us.

To be content with what one has is the greatest and truest of riches.

— Cicero

If you ever had the opportunity to see Robert Byrd orate on the House or Senate floor, you know how impossible it is to keep from feeling inspired. What a true patriot.

In May of 2005, he spoke to rebuke the ruling Republican Party in the Senate, who were engaged in a land grab of judicial nominations, and, after 208 of 218 were confirmed, they still held up Congressional business, demanding confirmation of the last ten, the most disturbing or extreme of the bunch.

Byrd drew from the Bible the story of Haman, who, along with his sons, was hanged on the gallows he himself had built. And Byrd quoted Tolstoy, and the story of Pahom, a greedy man who was offered all the land he could cover in a day for 1000 rubles. In the end, trying to cover too much land on foot, he collapsed by sundown, and ultimately earned himself a six-foot by three-foot piece of land – six feet deep with a headstone. Byrd asked the leader of the Senate, "How much land do you need?"

From the actual transcript:

"MR. INHOFE (R-Okla): 'Let me just make one answer on the question you had, how much more land? I refer to Jabez, you are familiar, in the First Chronicles. They say, expand my territory. *So we want more.*"

CHAPTER 3

America's Team? – May 16, 2005

What if your favorite sports team was powerful enough that it could use its influence to modify the league rules in its favor? Would you still stand behind them? Or would you stand up for what is right and fight for fairness?

Today there's a team that's bringing about an unprecedented revolution on the playing field of America. You haven't seen their games unless you catch them on C-SPAN. Let's give them a chic soccer name like the RNC Senators.

The Senators are emerging as the most powerful team in America. They already have a sizable base of fans whose parents supported them four decades ago, when they were quite a different team. Now they're a highly-motivated, well-organized, hardnosed bunch who have plenty of cash to throw around. They can find and recruit the best players, and pay them more money than the Yankees and Red Wings combined.

The Senators hold enough press conferences and televised rah-rah sessions to feed Big Media all they need to fill their half-hour spin shows. And because the papers are now calling them America's Team, the Senators are gaining fans across the entire U.S., even though those bandwagon fans know little about the team's traditions, little about how the game is played, little about the rules and bylaws, and little about the honored traditions of the game.

So after a couple of winning seasons, an ongoing propaganda campaign, the infusion of cash, and a rude, in-your-face approach, this team has gained newfound power. This power has allowed the Senators to do some amazing things.

First, they were able to fill the league rules committee with members of their own management. This allowed them to have an extraordinary amount of influence over the nomination and confirmation of umpires.

Second, they have been able to get away with having ethically-challenged players on their team who are regularly investigated for playing dirty, violating rules, and covering up their transgressions.

Thankfully there are still some umpires who are not afraid to stand up to the team manager when he marches out to protest a call. But the Senators have built up enough influence to call the commissioner and have the umpire overruled. After the game, they convene the rules committee, change the rule, and denounce the umpire in the press as un-American and call for his impeachment.

As the rich get richer, so power begets power, and that's set to happen with this bunch. You see, what they really want is to turn the league into a one-team system. Soon they'll revise the schedule so they play all their games at home. Tie games will be decided by an up or down vote, with their manager casting the deciding vote. They're already seating opposing fans behind soundproof glass so they can't be heard.

What's most amazing is that true sports fans are not incensed by this. Their gut feelings say it's wrong, their intellect confirms it's wrong. But if these Senators are getting away with it, they think maybe it's not our place to criticize.

For some people, a large part of their self-esteem is tied into being an RNC supporter. They'll tell you that "you have to stand for something, or you'll fall for anything." They stand for tradition; open-mindedness is considered a weakness.

But they don't grasp that tradition has already been thrown out the window. Wake up! These are not your father's Senators! Any true fan, any true lover of this American institution, would stand up and say, "Stop this now or you lose my support!"

Accumulating wins at the expense of integrity is wrong. We all should be talking about abiding by the rules, rules written over two centuries ago by our Founding Fathers, rules meant to protect a fragile system of government that many say can't last. These arrogant Senators want to make changes for the gain of their own team, not for the benefit and long-term strength of the system.

If these were my Senators, I would dump them and find a different party.

'...modern America, with its dominant urban culture, has now passed small towns by, relegating them to the cruel obscurity that comes from being abandoned by a railroad or left off the federal interstate highway map.' The casual visitor to most of these towns will note this decay immediately. Central business districts are devastated, shopfronts are boarded up, and both streets and once elegant houses are in advanced states of disrepair.

It is those features not automatically apparent to casual visitors that constitute the real tragedy of modern small-town life. Populated primarily by the elderly and by families attracted by the cheap rents, towns of less than 10,000 have larger concentrations of the poor, on a percentage basis, than cities do. Health care is generally inadequate, and both underfunded schools and social services are severely taxed, while domestic abuse, substance abuse, and teenage pregnancy are on the rise...

– Amy Greenberg, "Babbitt Who? The Decline of Small-Town America," *Reviews in American History*, Vol. 27, No. 2 (June 1999), p. 267-274.

When morning comes to Morgantown, the merchants roll their awnings down,
the milk trucks make their morning rounds in morning Morgantown.
We'll rise up early with the sun to ride the bus while everyone is yawning
and the day is young in morning Morgantown.

Morning Morgantown – buy your dreams a dollar down.
Morning any town you name, morning's just the same.

We'll find a table in the shade and sip our tea and lemonade
and watch the morning on parade in morning Morgantown.
Ladies in their rainbow fashions, colored stop and go lights flashing,
we'll wink at total strangers passing in morning Morgantown.

I'd like to buy you everything – a wooden bird with painted wings,
a window full of colored rings in morning Morgantown.
But the only thing I have to give to make you smile, to win you with
are all the mornings still to live in morning Morgantown.

– Joni Mitchell, *Morning Morgantown*, © Siquomb Publishing Company

CHAPTER 4

Small Town Values – June 15, 2005

One day during that last spell of hot weather, I walked up Main Street. Chelsea Office Supply was empty; someone was sweeping the decades of dust and memories out onto the steps and into a dustpan. I don't know that we could have saved that business, but we can save the others if we want. We should make it a point to do our shopping in downtown Chelsea.

A lot of people are putting a lot of effort into revitalizing downtown Chelsea, and it's time for all of us, if we honestly want to protect small town values, to act to make sure those efforts are not wasted.

Chelsea's charm leapt out at my wife and me the first day we strolled down Main Street, one summer in the mid-1990s. We met Sam in the hardware store, tiptoed through the McKune House, and poked our heads into the quaint office supply shop. The smell, the toys, the creaky wooden floor brought me back to the downtown stores of my childhood, in the 1960s, where the shopkeepers gave us kids lollipops and knew my mother by name.

You can walk up and down Chelsea's streets and find as many signs of good old American values as you want. The classic brick buildings and Victorian architecture. The clean downtown sidewalks. Flowers in a window basket. The friendly little firehouse. Barber shops, the post office, a corner grocery, a candy store, florists, gifts, and cafes. Two respected jewelers, a renowned bookstore, a nationally known theater, and a five star restaurant. And places to buy dress shoes, clothes, school supplies, or a pair of cowboy boots. Let's not forget the farmer's supply store that, thanks to genial Ben behind the counter, is a lot more fun than Tractor Supply or Lowe's, and overstuffed with dog food, fertilizer, cucumber seeds, grain, bird feeders, and baby ducklings, chicks, and turkeys.

Our world is changing. Clinging to these Norman Rockwell images can feel futile. But it can also motivate us to work to retain our small town charm.

What do we need to do?

For starters, we can't be free riders. We can't expect Chelsea to provide its charm to us without us giving back.

When I worked for General Electric one summer in 1985, they gave us t-shirts that said, "GE is Me." Like a church, or a club, or a school, or a business, Chelsea is us. We keep our own values alive by living them every day. We keep our town alive by living these values every day.

You don't join a rowing crew to take part in the camaraderie, the discipline, and the thrill of gliding across still water, but not the rowing. You have to become a contributing part of that team.

Small towns are failing, largely because we thoughtlessly pursue short-term self-interest. We make poor day-to-day choices. We can drive all the way out to Wal-Mart, Sam's, or Meijer and save a few quarters. But when we do, we drive another hole in the hull of our small town, all the while chatting about how we'd like to see Chelsea stay afloat.

Some of our shops, like Chelsea Market, prosper by providing products and services that the mega-marts can't. For example, large grocers create niches for the small because they can't provide local, top quality meats, prime deli services, or fine choices of wine and the expertise to go with it like little Chelsea Market can.

Others, like Vogel's and Foster's, thrive by offering quality clothing and great service like special orders and attentive, friendly salespeople who know their stuff.

On the other hand, Chelsea Office Supply was doomed with the advent of Staples and Office Depot. Office supplies are now commodities, and the big/online stores will win the battle both on selection and price. As for the chance to make it up with customer services, gone are the days when you might be able to bring a piece of office equipment back to the store if there were problems. Nowadays you send it to the manufacturer. (Or go to Circuit City and face the blank stare of some unfeeling, pimply-faced kid in Returns who's more worried about getting his smoke break than about your problem.)

We also lost A Gathering Basket. And Cranesbill Books. But we should have been able to keep those shops alive. We just needed to make a pointed effort to explore and shop in Chelsea.

The local stores continue to be enterprising – just drop downtown on a Thursday night. They could do a better job communicating to us what they offer. And they need to continue to produce value in the form of great service, great quality, and, most important to me, a friendly, welcoming atmosphere (read the memo, Chelsea Hardware). In return, it's up to us to patronize the downtown shops. We must think downtown first. And don't assume it means going out of your way. Collectively, downtown Chelsea is like a mini mall. Without the Disney Store. (I see that as a good thing.)

Start this week. Set aside one day and explore your Chelsea. Have brunch at a café. Do some shopping and some exploring. You'll be surprised at all you find, from Shoe Goo to Cajun peanuts, to massage artists, to Michigan Chillers, to CDs, to gourmet chocolate, to fine furniture.

Everyone's talking about values these days. Let's quit talking and live ours. Head downtown at least once a week with your shopping list in hand, before you make that trip out to Jackson Road.

The wise are instructed by reason; ordinary minds by experience; the stupid, by necessity; and brutes by instinct.

– Cicero

As you can imagine, I was not a fan of the George W. Bush presidency.

I tried not to hammer him every week, although I could have and I wanted to. In fairness, he did have some very low approval ratings, he shows up on several "worst presidents ever" Internet lists (in a 2009 HNN poll, sixty-one percent of historians rated the Bush presidency the worst ever), and critical world-altering decisions he made put us directly into the dire situation in which we find ourselves now.

If you are a fan of GWB, and you still believe Saddam had WMD, skip this one.

CHAPTER 5

Speech? What Speech? – June 30, 2005

In a past column I called Bush supporters and conservatives "the stupid masses." I've been waiting for a chance to apologize. So today, let me say I'm sorry for that. A more accurate term might have been stubborn masses. Masses unwilling to recognize the obvious.

Now those masses are dwindling. Those masses are starting to get the picture. The approval rating is down. Social Security privatization is dead. And President Bush's last national address (do you remember it?) drew the smallest TV audience of his term.

Bush's last speech was another rerun, an attempt to urge the American people to stand firm, to be patient, that we are making progress, that we must "complete the mission." Haven't we been hearing that for three years? Wasn't Mission Accomplished already declared with Bush's staged photo op on the USS Abraham Lincoln back on May 1, 2003?

I could sit here, as could many of my masses of non-stubborn, non-closed-minded, non-gullible friends, and say I told you so. I told you there were no WMD in Iraq. I told you Mr. Bush wanted to invade Iraq simply to get his revenge on Saddam. (Why did we need the Downing Street documents to prove that?) I told you Iraq and Osama were not connected, which we have known all along. I told you going into Iraq would create a civil war there. And I told you starting a fight against terrorism was like shooting a shotgun into a forest of beehives.

Before our invasion, Saddam ruled Iraq with the proverbial iron fist. No terrorist could thrive there. And the borders were closed. President Bush has turned Iraq into a hotbed for terrorism. And 1,700 of our soldiers have died trying to complete his mission, which has nothing to do with lofty ideals like defending America. Tragically, there was never really anything to defend America from.

Please don't suggest that I don't support the troops. I'm deeply thankful for their sacrifice. They should be home with their families like we are.

The good thing is that America is finally getting it. Not because anyone was stupid (and for that past implication I apologize dearly – never write a letter while you're angry) but because we, as a country, are finally starting to allow the tough questions to be asked. We no longer believe it when we're told it's unpatriotic to question the government. We're not afraid to stand up to a president who says, over and over, "Really, only patriots can see my clothes. Anyone who can't see them is un-American." As well as, "We're making progress. We're turning the corner. And being president is hard work."

In his speech, the president said his top job is to protect American life. Imagine if we had not invaded Iraq. There would still be no threat. Saddam would be under our thumb. Or dead, singly, if we had just sent in some Navy Seals. And we would have about $200 billion to use building our own roads and schools. What's not patriotic about that?

The president continues to talk about a global war on terror. That's as oxymoronic as a war on stupidity or a war on stubbornness. You can't declare war on an idea. You can only fight dangerous ideas with education and example. Israel has been fighting a war against terrorism for years and years. Have they made any progress? Have the Palestinians stopped their suicide bombing? Now in Iraq, the insurgents are saying they won't stop blowing themselves up until we leave the country. And the president is saying we won't leave the country until the insurgents quit blowing themselves up. Who wins? Other than Halliburton and the Bush/Cheney machine's corporate pals, no one. Without listening, without educating, without setting an example of understanding and peace, we just keep making more enemies, cultivating more and more terrorists worldwide.

The last time anyone suggested a peaceful approach, the administration bluntly told us, "You can't negotiate with terrorists." Ehm, why not?

Oh, wait a minute. We just found out from CNN that we have been negotiating with the Iraqi terrorists after all.

Keep your minds open. Don't swallow the lies. What's wrong with trying to get at the truth?

Let's all become enlightened masses – together.

It is a great thing to know our vices.

— Cicero

It's also a good thing to understand the Law of Unintended Consequences:

>Arizona's 'Support Our Law Enforcement And Safe Neighborhoods Act' is a losing wicket.
>
>The new law is good (if repugnant) Republican politics in Arizona because it turns on the party's anti-immigrant base.
>
>Perversely, it's good progressive politics. Kris Kobach has done for the state of Arizona what he did for a small suburb in Texas: drafted legislation that will transfer the state's wealth into the accounts of the Mexican American Legal Defense and Education Fund and the American Civil Liberties Union, whose legal staffs are already preparing lawsuits.
>
>The 'Support Our Law Enforcement And Safe Neighborhoods Act' might well have been called 'The Full-Employment Act for Civil Rights Lawyers.' A week after the Arizona governor signed it, it had been amended once and two lawsuits had already been filed.

– *Washington Spectator*, Volume 36, Number 9, May 15, 2010.

CHAPTER 6

Other Vices – August 15, 2005

My forties are going to be a struggle. I need to start taking care of myself. Both my dad and his dad had heart attacks in their forties. So I'm motivated. And yet I'm not doing it.

I'm only human, I guess.

I've cultured my bad habits over four decades. We all have our share of vices. Why don't we suck it up and live our values instead of just talking about them? We sure expect it from the other guy.

Remember the offensive editorial cartoon from a few weeks ago? Its message was that those lazy, greedy Mexicans should quit coming here to leech off America. The negative depiction of Hispanics was in complete opposition to reality. It painted a disturbing and unfair stereotype. It ignored the real world of the individual, a human being like you or me, with heart, ambition, desires, pressures, and shortcomings. It asked no thought questions. How many immigrants come here innocently, knowing nothing about America other than its promise to be the land of opportunity? How many simply want a chance to find a job, work hard, and build a future for their family?

What would you do in the same position?

It's so much easier to stereotype immigrants as lazy leeches, scheming over how to cross the border and squat in America and sign up for welfare. But we both know that's not the truth. It's just easier to wrap your head around.

What about all those other despicable factions of society? How easily we expect them to live up to our ideals, when we ourselves can't.

Those gays – they ought to resist that lifestyle. How many of us married men would be able to resist a come-on by a pretty woman? Don't kid yourself now.

Drug users – they ought to kick the habit and get clean. Tell that to Rush Limbaugh. After a certain point, it's not a choice. I can't even quit chocolate.

Teens – just say no, right? Abstain. Simple solution. Apparently you were never a teen. At sixteen, my brain may have said no, but my body said let the testosterone flow! Now, at forty, many of my hormones have flown – away. It takes two Viagra just to get me to take my wife out to dinner. And yet we can't even abstain from ogling scantily clad bodies on the Web.

Pick your pet demographic – minorities (Learn "our" language!), the poor (Get off welfare!), the inner city youth (Stand up to the gangs!). Then look in the mirror. Do you smoke? Pot? Abuse alcohol? Surf porn, cheat, gossip, overeat? Fudge your taxes? Ever collected unemployment? Food stamps? Social Security? Get a divorce? The guy in my mirror would fail to live up to any of the ideals we set for anyone else.

Real tolerance is about admitting that when we discriminate, we are discriminating not against stereotypes, but against real people – the bright-eyed immigrant who hopes to find honest work in America; the kid who has to join a gang or be ganged-up on; the single mother working two minimum wage jobs, with no time to study for a degree, and rising child care costs and rent. Where's the American Dream for these folks, people who weren't born into the middle class like me, or the now aristocratic upper class?

Real tolerance is about opening your mind and your heart, and not just on Sunday mornings flanked by your middle class, mainstream friends.

Look into the mirror. Are you afraid? Of what? Or are you too lazy like me?

It's easier to cling to our old bigotry. It's easier to remain closed to the truth. It takes less thought. And thinking is literally one of the hardest things for each of us to do!

Almost as hard as quitting smoking. Resisting the smell of McDonald's. Giving up chocolate.

Oh well, I guess we're all human.

Republican Joe Schwarz was the Seventh District U.S. Congressional Representative during the 2005-2006 session.

He was a decent moderate, very popular, and I liked him. I wrote the next column about him.

A few months later I wrote one that was unflattering and critical of Schwarz, inadvertently assisting Tim Walberg, an anti-abortion protester from Chicago, who was "tea party before tea party was cool." Walberg won the Seventh District seat in 2006 on the strength of a fired-up population of rural folks from the Wild West side of Washtenaw County. In the 2007-2008 session, Walberg passed no legislation other than one bill to rename a post office. Otherwise he is a "rank-and-file Republican" according to GovTrack, meaning he voted with his party and with George Bush practically every time.

A friend of a friend of mine, Mark Schauer, ran for the seat in 2008, and won it mostly on the wave of hope and change. The race was too close to be comfortable, and the Western Washtenaw Democrats played a key part in bringing out scale-tipping west-end votes for Schauer, Obama, and other Democrats in the election.

Walberg retook the seat in 2010 on the backs of the Tea Partiers.

Here's my initial column about Joe Schwarz.

CHAPTER 7

The Candy Parade – September 5, 2005

There were no babies to kiss, no hands to shake, no bumper stickers to pass out. It was just the Chelsea Fair parade – or what my kids lovingly call the Candy Parade – and all Representative Joe Schwarz had to do was stroll down the street, make sure he didn't get any melted Tootsie Roll on his shoes, and smile and wave.

He looked like he had gotten out of bed too early, like he knew he was in a parade but not which town, like his mind was on vacation. The smile was there, the wave was there, the head turn from one curb to the other was there. But Joe was out cutting grass on the back forty with Brett Favre.

That's when I stood up.

Never passing up an opportunity to embarrass my family, I rose from my lawn chair and called out to Mr. Schwarz. "Are you going to protect our Alaskan Refuge?" Politely, of course.

I stopped him in his tracks. Suddenly the grass was cut, the mower put away, and Joe was back in the office. He became Representative Joe Schwarz, of Michigan's seventh district.

Schwarz is a Republican, but an anomaly, not cut from the current "neo-con" cloth of big-corporation loving, take over all branches of government at any cost, forget any American who's not making over $250,000 per year Congressional right-winger. He's a moderate. He's against abortion, but supports women's rights. He accepts that some tax increases are fair and necessary. As a surgeon, he supports health care accessibility and embryonic stem cell research.

The Arctic National Wildlife Refuge is a vast stretch of pristine wilderness, a living reminder that conserving nature is a core American value. Sadly, oil taken from the Refuge would take ten years to get to market and would never equal more than two percent of our daily consumption. Sacrificing this jewel would do nothing to reduce gas prices or reduce our dependence on Middle East oil.

There's a greater reason Republicans want to unlock the Arctic Refuge. They know it would open the door for their Big Energy friends to invade our other wild places – the western canyonlands, ancient forests, coastal waters, and national monuments. "It's about precedent," Republican Congressional leader Tom DeLay admitted when he said this battle is really a fight over whether energy exploration will be allowed in similarly sensitive areas in the future.

There are only drips and dribbles of oil in those small, pristine pockets, but the energy companies know that we will pour millions of dollars in incentives their way as they explore, and much of that money will find its way to the pockets of the CEOs and board members.

Standing in the middle of the street, a gang of scooter-riding Shriners bearing down on him, Representative Schwarz put a hand to his ear.

"Are you going to protect our Alaskan Wildlife Refuge?" I called out, louder.

He looked me straight in the eye and said, "I will never vote for drilling in the Alaskan National Wildlife Refuge. Never." He was dead serious.

I gave him a wide smile and a thumbs up, and he strolled on, more resolutely now, symbolically treading just right of the center of the street.

Now there's a Republican even I can like.

The people's good is the highest law.

— *Cicero.*

CHAPTER 8

In Praise of Robert Byrd – September 16, 2005

I used to delete C-SPAN from my channel lineup. Then I started pausing there while channel surfing. Then I started watching it. Then I started to TiVo it.

If you didn't catch Senator Robert Byrd's Constitution Day speech this week, you don't realize what you missed. It was more timeless than even a Seinfeld rerun.

Robert Byrd is eighty-seven years old. He looks like Mr. Bean's grandpa, and is just as endearing. He's the longest-serving current member of Congress, having first been elected in 1953. Byrd is literally a walking encyclopedia on the history of the Senate, the Constitution, and Roman style of law. Back when the Republicans were planning to use a parliamentary trick to change the rules of the Senate in their favor, Byrd spoke out at length about the revered history that would be defiled. I have the video filed under "great historical speeches."

Robert Byrd is an incredible patriot, the right kind of patriot.

Byrd's Constitution Day speech was riveting as well, and it is especially relevant today as we ponder one political party's bid to take over all three branches of government. They have the Presidency; they have both houses of Congress; and they are poised to control the Judiciary with the next Supreme Court appointment.

Why is this bad? Because today it's the Republicans wresting power – and tomorrow it may be the Democrats. In twenty years, it could be the Libertarians, Greens, Radical Right, or Reform Party. In forty years, it could be the American Nazis, the Socialists, the Fascists, the Communists, or the Taliban. Unless we protect the balance of power.

Our Constitution prescribes it to assure us our freedom from oppression, to guarantee our fabled government "by the people and for the people" – not "by the rulers and for the rulers."

Or so the Founders intended. Google "absolute power corrupts." (And/or "Karl Rove, The Architect.")

Protection of the Constitution is Bird's passion, and Constitution Day is Byrd's Day. He introduced the bill creating the day. It is because of Robert Byrd that that lessons on the Constitution are to be provided in every school each September 17th. All my kids came home on Friday with some new Constitutional knowledge running around in their heads.

It's relevant that a federal judge last week declared the reciting of the Pledge of Allegiance in public schools un-Constitutional because of the words "under God." It apparently violates the rights of pupils to be "free from a coercive requirement to affirm God."

Crazy, right?

But stop and think. I go to church myself. About half of Americans do, and about two-thirds of us are religious. But if we must say "under God" when we pledge our patriotism, then down the road we may well find ourselves saying "under Allah"; or Brahma, Vishnu, or Siva; or Izamani and Izanagi; or Mohammed or Buddha or Confucius. Or Halliburton, OPEC, the Whig Party, Microsoft, NATO, you name it. Pledging our allegiance to our country, with the condition that we do it under a specific deity or force, is for certain unconstitutional!

Un-Constitutional.

Note that "under God" was only tacked on in 1954, after a vigorous campaign by special interest groups turned the Pledge into a public prayer as well as a patriotic oath.

Regardless of your religion, regardless of your political persuasion, you should not rejoice when your party wins absolute power, nor when your god becomes the official god of America. Because it will be someone else's next time. The worm will turn.

Learn about your Constitution. Respect it. And vote to protect it next time around. We need people like Byrd in office. We need to keep special interests out of the base rules of government. We need to rein in the political power-grab of the Right.

We The People need to restore the balance of power.

Ironically, the recently-elected gang of Tea Party and Republican governors and congressmen claim to be "strict Constitutionalists" and espousers of "less government," and yet they would change the Constitution in multiple ways if they could find a quill pen and a dark room. For example, Rick Perry, Texas governor and Republican presidential candidate, cites the seven ways he would actually overhaul the Constitution in his book *Fired Up!*

Among them:
- Suppress the power of the courts.
- Take away the freedom to elect our own U.S. senators.
- Reduce the freedom to marry by narrowly defining marriage.
- Reduce women's freedom of choice and control of their bodies.

It's interesting that they go up in a balloon proclaiming their goal of keeping government out of our lives…except when there are issues that they want their government to force onto the American people.

Power and law are not synonymous. In truth they are frequently in opposition and irreconcilable. There is God's Law from which all equitable laws of man emerge and by which men must live if they are not to die in oppression, chaos, and despair. Divorced from God's eternal and immutable Law, established before the founding of the suns, man's power is evil no matter the noble words with which it is employed or the motives urged when enforcing it. Men of good will, mindful therefore of the Law laid down by God, will oppose governments whose rule is by men, and if they wish to survive as a nation they will destroy the government which attempts to adjudicate by the whim of venal judges.

— *Cicero.*

CHAPTER 9

On Cronyism – October 3, 2005

The future of America, and the loss of your rights, are both being decided right now. You ought to care.

Here's how politics works today. Aspiring politicians need money to get elected. They get that from their political party, which woos powerful and wealthy interests in order to get the money they need to buy TV ads for candidates who support their political philosophies. The elected candidate is then bound to serve the party, and thus the interests that got him there. Anything the Congress or president appears to do for you is really a side effect of doing something for the party or the donors.

The House and Senate are not there for you. The president is not there for you. Whom does that leave? The third arm of government, the courts. They are the last – in fact, these days, the only remaining – line of defense for you and your freedom.

Last November, all we cared about, thanks to the political spin machines, was whether Roe V. Wade would survive, and whether gays would be able to marry. What a couple of red herrings. Who cares these days?

What if you lost your house in a storm, but your insurance company wouldn't pay? Or your IRA fund tanks because executives stole the money? Your employer takes away your pension? Or your local election has nineteen voting machines for registered Democrats and six machines for Republicans? What are you going to do?

You've got the court system to restore what's fair. You can go as high as the Supreme Court – the nine greatest legal minds in the country – nine impartial individuals who are above the political landscape, concerned only with interpreting the Constitution and applying the Bill of Rights on behalf of the little guy.

Wait a minute. Problem here. The Supreme Court is being populated by the most politically motivated administration ever.

Their blatant cronyism is not news, although there's a great article in last week's Time magazine about it. Katrina showed us that Michael "Brownie" Brown, whose primary job experience was as commissioner of the International Arabian Horse Association, was a Bush insider with political clout but no ability to handle the job as head of FEMA.

The administration's got us sufficiently frightened about Homeland Security. So we should have experts in there, right? We've got Julie Myers nominated to head Immigrations and Customs Enforcement (ICE). Her job will be to prevent terrorists from getting into the U.S. Myers is only thirty-six years old. Her current job? Special assistant for President Bush. She's married to Homeland Security Secretary Michael Chertoff's chief of staff (and recently away on honeymoon). Her uncle is the chairman of the Joint Chiefs of Staff. She was part of Ken Starr's team that attempted to roast Clinton for petty offenses. Is she qualified to head ICE? Maybe not, but she sure is connected.

Are you concerned about drug prices? Price gouging? Drug safety? Second rank at the FDA is Scott Gottlieb, ex-fellow at the American Enterprise Institute, a conservative think tank and supplier of warm, right-wing bodies to the Bush administration. There Gottlieb befriended Mark McLellan, who became FDA director in 2002. Recognize the last name? Mark McLellan is the brother of White House spokesman Scott McLellan, often seen squirming in front of the glaring press conference lamps on C-SPAN.

Gottlieb's key experience was as a pharmaceutical stock picker, with his own blog and newsletter. In those vehicles, he was a fierce critic of the FDA's slow approval process and consumer-protectionist approach to safety. When he became an FDA deputy commissioner, he had to recuse himself from taking part in deliberations involving major drug companies like Proctor & Gamble, Eli Lilly, and Roche because of his financial ties with them.

While the Florida votes were still being counted in 2000, Dick Cheney and Karl Rove were planning the most massive overhaul of government in history, as part of Rove's lifelong dream. Everyone in every nominatable position would be a person who supported Rove's neo-conservative ideals – the retention of wealth and power by the wealthy and the powerful.

And it's worked, and we have allowed it to happen.

Thankfully, the Supreme Court is our last bastion of freedom, of protection against this unabashed cronyism, right?

On Monday, President Bush nominated someone to replace the departing Sandra Day O'Connor. Her name is Harriet Miers. Certainly, she must be one of those "greatest legal minds" I talked about earlier, someone with no political ties, right? Wrong. Harriet Miers was Bush's Assistant and Staff Secretary when he was first inaugurated, his Deputy Chief of Staff in 2003, and Counsel to the President now. Harriet Miers is a lawyer who tells Bush how far he can go without getting impeached.

Harriet Miers has never even been a judge.

> *Exxon Mobil made $19 billion in profits in 2009. Exxon not only paid no federal income taxes, it actually received a $156 million rebate from the IRS, according to its SEC filings.*
>
> *Bank of America received a $1.9 billion tax refund from the IRS last year, although it made $4.4 billion in profits and received a bailout from the Federal Reserve and the Treasury Department of nearly $1 trillion.*
>
> *Over the past five years, while General Electric made $26 billion in profits in the United States, it received a $4.1 billion refund from the IRS.*

– Michael Mechanic, "Bernie Sanders' Top Ten Tax Avoiders," *Mother Jones*, March 29, 2011. Note that these numbers are certainly cherry picked, and misleading enough to make things sound sufficiently egregious. Of course, these companies paid taxes; but we have heard and read enough factual reports to understand that these companies defraud the US out of billions in tax dollars through dozens of types of shelters and hedges, not the least of which is through accounting: shifting income overseas to avoid paying US taxes, and getting tax credits for doing it!

Here's another op-ed that translates well over the years. It has been interesting to watch the price of gas rise and the sales volume of SUVs shrink. And the price of gas fall, and the sales of SUVs rise.

CHAPTER 10

The Big (Oil) Ten – October 17, 2005

Out here on the vast, windswept plains along the Washtenaw-Jackson county border, we're hoping for a mild winter. The Michigan Public Service Commission says natural gas prices will be up about fifty percent this season. We're secretly thinking global warming might not be all that bad after all. At least for us.

Thankfully, Michigan utilities do not profit on the natural gas they sell us – they make their bucks on the "delivery service" – so they can't price gouge on the product itself. Governor Granholm last week reminded the state's natural gas suppliers that they'll be under the magnifying glass during the coming season; the MPSC will be watching to make sure price increases are reasonable, appropriate, and legal.

This is the same Jennifer Granholm who joined with twenty-seven state governors in a non-partisan bid to get Congress to provide energy assistance funds for the states that will need them most in the next months; it was defeated in the U. S. Senate by two votes.

I know what you're saying. "There he goes again, bringing national politics into this."

But hey, you have to admit, the contrast is compelling. For example, the feds give us lip service about looking into price gouging at the gas pumps, months after our tanks and wallets are dry. But nothing happens. "No evidence of price gouging was found." How? By whom?

Meanwhile, the Governor is doing the right kinds of things here in our back yard. In September, she phoned the president of

Marathon Oil and asked him to lower Marathon's gasoline prices. He promptly lowered them by forty cents a gallon.

Of course, Granholm can do that because she's not in bed with the petroleum industry.

The Big Oil Ten made more than $100 billion in profits last year. Every time they raise their prices, they tell us that supplies are tight because we don't have the refining capacity. Case in point: this winter's coming price increases are blamed on the damage Katrina and Rita did to refineries in Louisiana and Texas. At the same time, the petroleum industry has been gradually shutting down refineries for thirty years. In that time, they have closed over half of them (although, to be fair, total refining capacity has dropped only a bit). There has not been a major new refinery built in the U.S. since 1976.

A phone call from Jennifer Granholm won't fix this one. She might dial up Lee Raymond, Chairman and CEO of Exxon, and urge him to invest some of those record profits in some domestic refineries. She'd have more luck asking him to invest some of his big bucks in some horizontal drilling under the Great Lakes. Raymond took home over $38 million in total compensation last year from Exxon, plus he cashed out $43 million in stock options, and still has $65 million in unexercised stock options stashed away in his strongbox.

Raymond would tell Granholm that refineries are unprofitable. He would tell her that it's too much trouble to build them in a way that safeguards local citizens, wildlife, waterfowl, game, waterways, air, and crops. And so on. He would tell her that it's easy enough getting our oil from refineries in the Middle East.

What he would not tell her is that when supplies are low, demand is high, and domestic refining capacity is the bottleneck, Big Oil can redouble their profits.

Maybe I'll buy a Hummer, convert it to solar power, and live in it until spring. Oh, and pray for a little global warming.

NEW YORK (CNNMoney) – The United States is awash in gasoline. So much so, in fact, that the country is exporting a record amount of it. The country exported 430,000 more barrels of gasoline a day than it imported in September, according to the U.S. Energy Information Administration.

The United States began exporting gas in late 2008. For decades prior, starting in 1960, the country used all the gas it produced here plus had to import gas from places in Europe.

"We've got plenty of excess refining capacity," said Jonathan Cogan, a spokesman for EIA. "It's a reminder that this is a global oil market, and it's reflected by the movements of products to where they will get the highest prices."

Still, the ability to export oil is good news for Shell and other oil companies like Exxon Mobil, BP, and Chevron. They can use their extensive and modern refineries in the United States to make gasoline for the rest of the world.

But it may be bewildering for American drivers, who could experience record high gas prices next year even though U.S. demand could hit the lowest level in a decade, said Tom Kloza, chief oil analyst at the Oil Price Information Service. "I can understand it, from a truck driver's perspective," said Kloza. "You're paying $4 or $4.50 a gallon to run your rig, yet we're exporting the crap out of this fuel. I'd be outraged too."

– excerpted and abridged, Steve Hargreaves, @CNNMoney, December 5, 2011

In October, I received a surprise email from Michelle, my editor. She pointed me to a political performance poll and asked me to have a look and to offer my analysis and opinion.

This writing later appeared just before the 2010 elections, in a revised, updated, and shortened form, in a mailing we sent to most Washtenaw County residents. It was a highly partisan piece, perhaps too much so.

"We needed to do two things – citizen responsibilities – and we need to do them now. We need to find out the truth about our elected officials. President Obama, like Granholm, does not promote his successes. He just quietly soldiers on, in my opinion trying to do what he believes is best for America. Mark Schauer fights for jobs and the people of southern Michigan, whereas Tim Walberg accomplished nothing for us while in office, and promises a return to the Bush policies. Excuse me, were you in a coma during the Bush years?

Let's not go back to 2004."

If you can read past the partisan tone, you'll catch that the article examines how public sentiment can have us voting with our knees and not with our brains.

The raw poll results are no longer available online or by request, and I could not find a copy on my computer, or I would have included them here.

CHAPTER 11

Political Performance Poll – October 31, 2005

Michigan likely voters were polled last week on the performance of our elected officials.

First the obvious conclusions.

On issues where the public is uninformed, we respond down party lines (forty-six percent Democrat, forty-two percent Republican). That seems bullheaded. In these times, we all ought to be "undecided" until someone can step up and prove they are the right person for the job, not just the right ideologue. We should have learned that from the 2004 election. Since the Inauguration, have we heard boo about any of the hotly-debated ideological issues we were tricked into focusing on?

Bush's approval ratings are at rock bottom. (Come on, you stubborn twenty-two percent who still approve, put aside your pride.) In a sick and twisted turn, Bush dumped his crony Harriet Miers, who was approved by forty-six percent of voters, because of the hell raised by the small faction of extreme right-wingers he considers his base. In a do-over like we used to give my little brother in kickball, Bush has appointed Samuel Alito, who's a lot more right-wing. I predict he'll get nowhere near forty-six percent approval here, not when fifty-six percent of us support women's rights (that's "freedom" by the way – do you value yours?) and Roe v. Wade, and the same number now realize Bush's brand of conservativism is nothing like Reagan's conservatism. If the Court becomes neo-con/teapublican, we'll all lose a measure of good old American freedom.

Finally, all incumbents in Michigan, and across the country, are at risk of being replaced. This is because we are uninformed about their performance. And, to be frank, they haven't shown results. Michigan seems no closer to solvency; and the U.S. Congress is a mess.

Next, the not so obvious conclusions.

Governor Granholm's approval rating is nearly as bad as Bush's. Really. Is she that unlikable? No. But she's an unknown. If she wants to convince us that we, as a state, are better off than we were when she was elected, she needs to blow her horn.

According to the Democratic Governors Association, Jennifer Granholm has resolved more than $4 billion in budget deficits, and chopped more money from state government than any governor in the state's history. Remember her bold move to reexamine every state contract in the last couple years? My full-time employer wasn't ultimately affected, but we sure took notice and trimmed the fat from our proposals.

She was responsible for "Jobs Today, Jobs Tomorrow" which created jobs by speeding up infrastructure projects, training unemployed workers, adding money to the Jobs for Michigan Fund, and reducing red tape for businesses that seek state permits. As a result, small firms grew by 2,400 last year. Seven companies opened new headquarters here. Direct action by the state created or retained 130,000 jobs. She attracted Toyota, which announced plans to invest $150 million in a new R&D facility in York Township, which will create over 600 new jobs.

In *Governing* magazine's "Grading the States 2005" report, only Virginia and Utah scored higher than the Granholm administration – in the areas of money, people, infrastructure, and information management.

Jennifer Granholm has saved us nearly $40 million in prescription drug costs while actually expanding health care coverage for the uninsured and needy. And this year, for the first time, classrooms in Michigan actually received the funding they were promised. And Granholm has been a major force in cracking down on gas station price gouging, and in successfully lobbying big oil companies to reduce their pump prices.

Finally, the subtle conclusions.

Two common threads weave through the poll results. First, we are not content with the economy nor the direction we are heading, whether it be with the Michigan economy, the changes to the Supreme Court, the war in Iraq, the deterioration of morals in the Republican Party, or the performance of the Congress. Second, we are uninformed about individual players, whether they be incumbents or potential candidates.

We need to do two things, and I consider these citizen responsibilities. We need to find out about our elected officials. Are Granholm, Stabenow, and Levin doing a good job, in spite of current overall conditions, or not?

And we need to examine the next wave of candidates with new criteria: what are their moral references? What have they accomplished? How will they help us on the pressing, relevant issues? Will they stay away from spin and smoke and mirrors on such red herrings as abortion, gay rights, affirmative action, terrorism, swift boat service, and so on? Can a Tea Partier or angry Republican actually govern? Or are we electing Jesse Ventura or Soupy Sales as a knee-jerk reaction to current events?

If you vote Democrat, find yourself a moderate, someone who will denounce abortion while protecting women's rights; someone who will stand up for hunters' rights while supporting gun control in the cities; someone who will assure us that America's many factions don't get special rights, but they do get full equal rights.

The Republican Party seems always to offer up only extremists. If you vote Republican, find yourself another Schwartz, not a mean-spirited, conniving "hammer" like Frist or Delay. We've had enough of the WWE version of the Republican Party, the rich and richer elite who want to take the entire left side of government and "drown it in the bathtub." Let's get back to the 1980 Olympic

Hockey Team version, where we all play together against the world, not each other.

At the heart of this poll is one message. Is your party representing you? Take a long hard look at yourself, and at what's really important today. How does your party represent that? The parties have changed a lot in the last twenty years.

It's time for all of us to reevaluate.

Doing the same thing over and over but expecting different results is a kind of insanity. Why on earth would we want to return to the Bush years? Rupert Murdoch and his Fox News have conditioned us all to respond to fear. Remember "terror levels?"

What we need to fear now is a return to the radical government we ushered in after 2010 – to the super-rich getting richer, the middle class declaring bankruptcy, and the poor filling the streets, homeless shelters, and prisons; to new military invasions across the world; to the loss of your Social Security benefits; to further loss of individual rights; to the nullification of contracts by governments; to greater and greater deficits; to diminished education and higher crime; and to massive corporate corruption and increasing corporate power over our elected officials.

A s of this writing, you can go to www.redcrossblood.org to find out about donating blood. There are two places to type in your ZIP code and find nearby blood drives or learn about your local Red Cross.

I like to donate because it's one of the few ways I'm giving back to society without shelling out more greenbacks, and I'm volunteering without the typical time commitment. To me, it's a fine opportunity to read or catnap.

At a blood drive in Chelsea a few years back, my blood-drawing angel Jane invited me to try something called Apheresis – or double red cell donation. I'll try anything, and so I did, and I have been donating double reds ever since. It's that good.

Apheresis is similar to a whole blood donation, except a special machine is used to allow you to safely donate two units of red blood cells during one donation. You get poked in the arm just the same, and then your blood goes into a little machine about the size of an old portable record player. The machine separates your blood with a centrifuge and keeps two units of red cells for itself, and then safely returns all the remaining blood components, along with some replacement saline to make you feel refreshed, back to you through the same arm. You don't lose the liquid portion of your blood, you feel more hydrated after your donation, and you feel better over the next couple days.

Double red cell donation takes about twenty minutes longer than a normal (whole blood) donation, but you only have to donate half as often – every four months. So if you are time-challenged, it's the way to go. It is as safe as whole blood donation. Just make sure that when you make your appointment, you tell them you want to donate double reds. And when you show up, remind them that you are donating double reds.

CHAPTER 12

Needles – November 14, 2005

I hate needles.

Wait. I used to hate needles. Now I'm a whole lot better at getting poked and not passing out, thanks to the Red Cross. It's one of the benefits of giving blood.

Now I just really, really dislike needles.

For a long time I never considered donating blood. To me it was something that other people did. Like diving, three meter or SCUBA. Watching rugby. Turning cartwheels. Sauna. Cross-country skiing. Scottish Highland Dance. Then I realized it would present a compelling challenge. I could find out whether I had the guts to go get poked for no good reason. And if I had the guts, then I might just overcome my needle anxiety.

After a couple gallons of blood over the years, I can truly say it's been a good idea. I can watch Grey's Anatomy without covering my eyes during the IV insertions. I can bandage my own cuts, even the deep ones like the one I got when I touched the spinning blade of my chop saw. Heck, if I were diabetic, I could probably even give myself my own insulin injections.

Meanwhile, I have learned a few other things. Donating blood is easy. It doesn't cost me anything – my boss gives me paid time off to go. And there's free food. The cookies and juice flow nonstop wherever you donate. Sometimes they're homemade. If you drive up to Delphi for one of their open drives, you'll get pizza. Honest!

You should donate blood. Yes. You. And you should do it again the next day you become eligible.

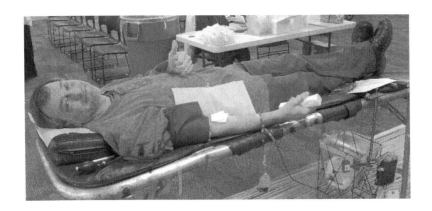

Donations drop over the holidays. People get busy. I don't know about you, but my warm, lazy autumn is quickly turning into a chaos of bow hunting, Christmas shopping, leaf raking, late season fence mending, Thanksgiving cooking (OK, eating and football watching), and holiday planning and travel. Forget the everyday stuff like work, exercise, family time....

As I get more and more busy, I find I have less and less time to give of myself to others. That is, I start taking time from others to give to myself. After this year's natural disasters, you've probably given a lot of yourself (and your cash) to the Red Cross and other charities. You probably feel a little tapped out right now. The good news is that giving blood is free. It costs us nothing but a little time.

During the winter holidays, our national blood supply literally runs short, down to something like one day. This is blood that's used by trauma victims (car accidents can require 100 pints of blood), babies, soldiers, your relatives, neighbors, and friends. Your blood is needed for heart surgeries (my dad), organ transplants (daughter of a co-worker), complications during childbirth (my wife), leukemia (my son's friend Andrew) and cancer patients (my friend Jayne's daughter), newborns and premature babies (all my kids).

Can you imagine your single pint of blood being used to save the life of one premature baby? To honor, to thank, to heal one soldier? To bring a kid with cancer one step closer to coming home from Mott and going back to school? It's not like donating a kidney. It's just a little Ziploc bag of your blood. To save someone.

Why not you?

According to the Red Cross, the main reason donors give blood is because they want to help others. The top two reasons people say they don't give blood are that they have never thought about it, and they don't like needles.

Well, now you've thought about it. You've been invited. Urged. Guilted, I hope.

And you'll get used to the needles. I did. As a matter of fact, I can barely wait until my fifty-six days are up and I can go get poked again. I don't even need to bring my teddy bear with me anymore.

You can find all you need at www.redcrossblood.org, or go straight to the website at www.wc-redcross.org for Washtenaw County open drives. You used to be able to call 800-GIVE-LIFE, although I don't see that number advertised on the website as of this writing. Or try 800-RED-CROSS, which is shown on the website.

Where is there dignity unless there is honesty?

— Cicero

Iraq Invasion Casualty Number 2101: Pfc. John W. Dearing
Died: November 21, 2005 in the Iraq invasion, when an improvised explosive device detonated near his HMMWV during combat operations near Habbaniyah.

Home: Hazel Park, Michigan

Age: Twenty-one years old

Unit: Army National Guard's 1st Battalion, 125th Infantry Regiment, Saginaw, Michigan.

J.W. was born on Sept. 10, 1984, the son of John and Kitty Dearing. He graduated from Oscoda High School in 2003. He loved baseball, NASCAR, bowling, and hunting.

"Country Boy, Country Boy, Country Boy. I could talk about him all day, and not run out of funny stories. We met on the journey here. We shared many a brew, and talked about everything under the sun. I was there that day, on the ground with everyone, scrambling to get the guys out. I'll never forget the emptiness I felt when I only counted four, not five that made it out. You were my best friend, and I'll watch over your family – for as long as I live. Save me a seat with a view man. I'll see you when I get there!"

Your Bro Jay of Habbaniyah Iraq (posted on fallenheroesmemorial.com)

CHAPTER 13

How Many More? – November 18, 2005

Seems like just last week we turned the corner, 2000 of our guys and girls dead in Iraq since we invaded. And now we're at 2100.

How many do you think will die before it's done? What will be the name of the next one to be killed? The names of his or her spouse, children, parents?

Regardless of how you feel about it, you have to admit: We're in a hell of a mess.

It's like when you're playing poker and you think you have a good hand, or a good bluff, and as you dump more and more into the pot, you start to realize you're not going to make it. You feel embarrassed. You secretly pray you won't have to show your cards. You think of the pile of cash you're going to lose. You feel sick to your stomach. And there's no turning back. You either keep feeding the pot you know is going to end up in someone else's lap, or you turn in your cards and take the loss.

When the hand was dealt, all you allowed yourself was a rosy image of getting a couple helper cards, declaring Mission Accomplished as you lay down your hand triumphantly, and raking in a hefty pot of capital. You never considered that you might lose. You never planned for that.

Right now the Democrats are talking about accountability, talking about a plan, talking about getting out. And the Republicans are trying to discredit the Democrats. "You voted for the invasion."

"Yeah, but we were lied to about the need for it."

Remember, it was never about terrorism. The 9/11 terrorists were Saudis, not Iraqis. It was about Saddam and his (non-existent) great big weapons. And President Bush's secret but obvious agenda.

I was dead set against this Iraq invasion. I'm also against the so-called War on Terror. To me, it's like living next to a forest full of hornets. You start getting stung, you plant some flowers on the far side of the woods. You don't start taking pot shots with your shotgun.

And don't fall for the baseless, "If we fight them over there, we don't have to fight them over here." That's simplistic, misapplied, and cowardly. God gave us brains to think for ourselves, not follow the advice of bumper stickers. Except for the chillingly correct, "We're making enemies faster than we can kill them."

We're in a hell of a mess. In Iraq we're fighting civilians, radicals, and not an opposing army. The same thing happened in Vietnam, and the orders eventually became "just kill everybody." We're not winning in Iraq.

Here's the problem: We can't walk away now.

I hate to say it, being a pretty strong believer in peace and goodwill. But if we walk away, we leave the country in total chaos, we let down the innocent people of Iraq, we hand them over to the radical factions fighting for control.

At least life under Saddam was predictable. Tell me again why we didn't just send in the Navy Seals, take him out, and set up a puppet government like we used to do under Nixon and Reagan?

It looks like the only real way to end this war is to try to get a real coalition, not W's "mother-of-all-coalitions" consisting of us, Mauritania, Kyrgyzstan, Belize, and French Somaliland. If we had any international political capital, and if we had a plan, and if we had some due dates, we could go to the rest of the world and put together a shocking, awesome military force to go in, finish this invasion, set up the government, and hand things over to the Iraqi people within a couple years.

We sure can't stay the course. Not when there is no course.
We can't pull out, not after what we've done.
We need to finish this thing.
We need to fold this hand and move on to the next deal.

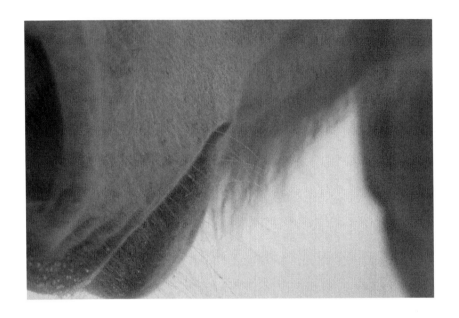

Equality of rights under the law shall not be denied or abridged by the United States or by any state on account of…[anything].

– *Equal Rights Amendment,* first introduced in 1923, approved by Congress in 1972, but not ratified by the necessary number of states, and thus never adopted.

CHAPTER 14

MLK – January 6, 2006

Next week Chelsea and all of America will celebrate Martin Luther King Jr. Day. The goal of the celebration is to promote recognition of the diversity of the human family, and understanding of the world's cultures.

This is the 20th year for the federal holiday. If you haven't gotten on board yet, I urge you to do so.

I grew up just a day's canoe paddle south of Lake Superior, in northern Wisconsin. The only racial diversity around me was the Native American influence that's still prevalent there. We mixed on the playground, a bunch of kids who knew no prejudice, other than what our parents tried desperately to instill in us. Every day I question whether I've truly been able to remain above that prejudice over the years.

On Monday I'll question whether I would have even tried, without the actions of people like King and the Civil Rights movement that followed. In truth, King represents the efforts of any group to stand up for their rights. Whether or not you sympathize with every group that feels discriminated against, you have to realize that in this country, in this America, of which we are so fond of saying we are proud, you need to have recourse when your rights are being violated, when your freedom is being taken away, because it happens all the time.

All sorts of rights are under attack these days: the right to vote, the right to speak freely, the right to own a gun, the right of sexual preference, your right to privacy, the right to have a clean environment, the right to demonstrate for peace, the right to control what your government spends your money on, your right to honest representation in government, the right to control your own body, your unborn child, your time of death, the use of your organs. (Add your own petitions here; I have only nicked the surface.)

If you feel the threat against any of these rights, then you should respect the acts of Martin Luther King Jr.

Seniors, whom do you have to stand up for you against unfair advertising, unconscionable drug company profits, and elder-care abuse?

Children, who stands for you when you're left behind by a school system short on funds because of a trillion dollar war?

Citizen, who stands for you when half your campaign contributions go to a lobbyist who supports your cause, and the other half to a lobbyist who fights against them? Who stands for you when the super-rich get richer, the super-rich get tax cuts, and the super-rich get to pass their growing riches down generation to generation so the American dream no longer works for anyone?

Who stands for the poor and needy, the genius born in the ghetto, the Olympian who can't afford shoes, the single-parent child with a working mother, no one home after school, and a gang selling drugs outside the front door?

We never saw any African Americans in the Great White North. Nor do we see a lot of racial diversity outside the bubbles of Ann Arbor and Ypsilanti. It's kind of hard to know how to embrace the diversity of the human family, to understand the world's cultures when it's always been defined as black skin and white skin, as represented by black American heroes and patriots like King and Rosa Parks.

The point is that Martin Luther King Jr. Day does not really have to be about the black and white divide. It's about the great leadership that one American provided for a group that was being denied the right to equality, the right to freedom, by America itself, against its very Constitution and the Founding Fathers who drafted it.

We each need to open up our hearts and minds to what the human family really means – it's a lot more than simply a melting pot of races – and what's meant by "the world's cultures."

We need more great leaders who'll stand up for those groups that are tread upon by those of us privileged few who think we're as moral as we can get, who think we're tolerant, giving, kind, generous, and understanding, who think we're not prejudiced.

On Monday, August 16, 2010, Politico reported that News Corp., the parent company of Fox News (and the New York Post, Wall Street Journal, and Times of London), made a $1,000,000 donation to the Republican Governor's Association. You couldn't ask for a clearer illustration of the circular handshake taking place between the Republican Party and Fox News. 'Fair and Balanced' news coverage feeds Republican power, which turns into more 'Fair and Balanced' news, with good government nowhere to be found.

– *ActBlue*, August 18, 2010.

CHAPTER 15

Chocolate Cake for Breakfast – January 23, 2006

Notes to self (*not* New Year's Resolutions): Keep it local. Don't ramble. Quit the liberal rants. Don't overuse parenthetical phrases and quotation marks. Stay within 500 words. Lose ten pounds.

Oops, that last one was definitely a resolution.

I'm not one for New Year's Resolutions. I'm fully able to make (and break) resolutions all year long. I can lose ten pounds in July just as well as in January. Either way, the pounds all come back by Christmas. Or should I say The Holidays?

Did you even notice how we made it safely through December unscathed by the fallout from this "Christmas controversy?" I guess showman Bill O'Reilly made his ratings by blowing the whole Happy Holidays thing into a War on Christmas. Funny, I've never heard any word about old Bill attending church himself. (If you can vouch for him, please email me.) Frankly, I have a hard time imagining him kneeling before anyone, even Jesus.

What's interesting when you start to think about local vs. non-local news and commentary is that it's less about what's happening in the village, and more about what affects us on an individual level.

The Detroit TV stations, for example, confuse the two. There's not a night when the lead story isn't about a bloody car crash or a drive by shooting. That may be local in the sense of locale, but is it really anything we care about? We're drawn to it like drivers are drawn to gape at a car accident on the freeway. When are the big TV stations going to figure out that "if it bleeds, it leads," as well as the annoyingly irrelevant "you heard it here first" are *so* 1940s. They went out the same door that television came in.

But I ramble. Back to Happy Holidays.

If you hadn't heard about the whole (non-)issue on O'Reilly or Limbaugh, you wouldn't even know there was a controversy. You wouldn't care. Those guys won again. They got us up in arms. They manipulated us. We were duped. Doesn't that bother you? It would bother me, except I got some great laughs off *The Daily Show* and Jon Stewart – who's really one of our great political talk show minds, and not just a loud mouth.

The point is, this clearly national issue did matter to some of us. I guess that was enough to make it local news.

Doesn't the same principle apply to the secret, illegal wiretapping business that's going on? That ought to matter to all of us. It's very likely that someone right here in the 'hood has been spied upon.

Don't believe me? How about those Florida Quakers? They found out their meetings were stored in the Pentagon's database of suspicious incidents. Think CANOPAS is immune? Think you're immune? The White House last week asked for several terabytes of Google search data so they could go through looking for porn surfers. Not terrorists. Google said, "No."

MSN won't tell us what they said when the government asked them. Meaning they have probably already handed over data to the government, and are probably doing it on a regular basis. So. Be honest with yourself. Ever searched for porn? Even soft porn? Even an itsy-bitsy, teenie, weenie, polka-dot bikini bit? Even once?

Is it local news now?

The Bush administration's story is that "we're only performing surveillance on the people we already know are bad." Excuse me? Then why set up wiretaps without getting a judge's approval first? I thought we were presumed innocent in America?

So Bush's and Cheney's alibis don't ring true. That should not surprise you, at least those of you who don't have your heads still buried under the "only Republicans can be Christians" sand of autumn, 2004. You're intelligent, proud, and skeptical enough to have figured out that little truth comes out of the White House, and it hasn't been coming out of there since January 20, 2001. (OK, OK, since about 1998, I admit, which is too bad. If it wasn't for a bubbly little brunette intern, we'd have Gore in the White House right now and we'd still be sitting on a huge budget surplus and a healthy economy. Iraq would still be terrorist free and have no weapons of mass anything worth worrying about. And we would have negotiated peace with Osama bin Laden.)

But I digress. And in the span of 500-odd words, I've successfully broken all those New Year's Resolutions.

Now, to top it off with a piece of chocolate cake for breakfast.

When Jennifer Granholm became the 47th Governor of Michigan in 2003, she inherited a massive budget deficit from Governor Engler. She successfully resolved over $14 billion in budget deficits her first year, through a significant number of budget cuts.

At the same time, she was upset by proposals to cut state funding to social welfare programs, and said this:

"Often those who cloak themselves in a cape of religiosity happen to be some who are the biggest cutters. Now, some of that can balance out. But when you get to cutting the services for the least of these – in the 25th chapter of Matthew in the 37th verse the Lord says, 'Whatsoever you do to the least of these, so also you do unto me' – that's when I question whether somebody is really living out the faith that they profess."

CHAPTER 16

In Support of Governor Granholm – February 6, 2006

If Governor Jennifer Granholm took the Bush approach to explaining her troubles, she'd grumble, "Being the Governor is hard work!" But in her State of the State speech, there were no violins, no whining. She looked to the future with optimism, and with a plan. Given what she inherited in 2003, and the tough conditions since then, you have to admire her tenacity and leadership.

Pitifully, the right half of the state legislature, grown men and women, remained in their seats like pouting children as Granholm unveiled plans that drew applause from the entire audience as well as the left side of the aisle.

Of course, it wouldn't be right for the Republicans to applaud the opposition, would it? That's not done these days. Apparently our good old American values have changed. "No comfort or aid" to the enemy, and now the enemy is anyone who doesn't think the way I do. (Case in point, the fallacious War on Christmas.) If it's not their idea, they're not going to support it, even if it does help the people of Michigan. They would rather it fail.

The Republicans in the Michigan Legislature are happy to beat the droll tin plate of tax cuts, like they always have. They know that the lower and middle class citizens in the state (like me) will bite on a $100 income tax break. Hey, I can buy twenty more lottery tickets this year (or go to another Day Trader Secrets seminar) in my continuing quest to get rich the only way possible anymore.

They also know that the small businesses that are profitable enough to qualify for the Single Business Tax (SBT) will bite as well. My brother-in-law tells me he can save over $16,000 next year if

Michigan eliminated the SBT. That'll buy him a new boat (likely built outside the state) or pad my niece's college fund for Stanford or Miami. It won't create a single job.

Oh, by the way, the SBT only kicks in after he's made $350,000. Are you subject to it?

I guess the good news for me is that I'll never have to pay it.

The theory is that reducing the SBT will draw more businesses (and hence jobs) to the state by improving our tax climate. But that's part of the old slippery supply-side mentality favored by the conservative side of government, who, conveniently, are friends to the rich, powerful, corporate crowd who stand to gain the most from tax cuts. Keep in mind that states like California, New York, and Massachusetts aren't suffering from the poor tax climates they offer to businesses.

The theory that lowering taxes will solve our economic problems is just that – a theory. It's one that's been proven just about as many times as Creationism; interestingly, its supporters are just as fervent. In fact, the tax theory has been repeatedly disproved. In *no case* has it ever been shown to work. There is *no relationship* between tax rates and job creation.

The opposing theory reflects the reality we see around ourselves every day: that no one is going to decline a raise just because their taxes will go up. I'd gladly hit the $350,000 mark in sales if I could. I'd frame my tax bill next to my diploma. I'd wear my tax burden like a badge of honor. I'd pay my tax bill with a smile, and laugh all the way to the bank with my leftover profits. Why wouldn't I?

When she took office, Governor Granholm was handed a huge budget deficit by Republican governor Engler. State revenues were falling. We were tapping into the rainy-day Budget Stabilization Fund (BSF). Interest on our debt was $470 million and growing. America was in a recession. Federal spending for luxuries (like the invasion of Iraq) cut funding to states. And we were saddled with a dinosaur of an industry in automobile manufacturing – and this year has shown us that the Age of Mammals is coming on fast.

No one should blame Jennifer Granholm if she lies down to sleep at night mumbling, "This sure is hard work." It's a job I'm not sure even I would want. And yet she's out with a smile on her face, a plan in her pocket, and the determination to continue working hard until the problems are fixed.

I admire that, and I trust that. And by the way, I trust it a lot more than another billionaire challenger, or a bunch of closed-minded, not-invented-here, obstructionist conservative fat cats, promising that a magic-dust sprinkling of tax cuts will solve everyone's problems.

I don't want your tax cuts. I want to make a good living, and in turn pay my fair share, and I want it applied where it will help us all in the long run – into early education that creates good citizens from the start; into infrastructure that prevents poverty and crime instead of punishing it after the fact; into help for poor parents who have to juggle multiple jobs, raising good kids, and going to school; into better roads (I spent my federal "tax cut" last year replacing two pothole-damaged tires); into better wages for our police and fire crews; and into fair health services for the poor.

I have faith that Granholm will keep us on the right path, with or without the help of the Republican side of the legislature.

The next writing was a guest column I did for the student newspaper where I taught classes part time. You don't really need the text of their article to understand what it said. I pretty much lay that out, and you can gather it in from the context.

CHAPTER 17

State of the Union Speech – February 8, 2006

While I applaud the upbeat tone of the recent staff editorial, I do not agree with its assessment of the State of the Union speech. Too much positive thinking is what's allowing a dishonest White House administration to take advantage of the American people, eat away at our rights, make us less safe than we've ever been, and feed record profits to the oil companies with a golden spoon.

President Bush was given the benefit of the doubt on most counts. But try looking at the issues from the opposite perspective: "What would an administration be doing if they were corrupt, if they were trying to take advantage of us?"

They might claim that the Patriot Act is necessary to "fight terrorism." And they might trump up terrorism into more than a threat than it really is. In fact, they might even hope for some continuing acts of terrorism in order to keep us afraid, and to keep our minds off the fact that every single time, in history, when wiretapping and spying have been used by an administration, they have been used to spy on enemies of the political party, not enemies of America. (To be fair, the editorial did echo my concern.)

You took no real position on the invasion of Iraq; in that regard, Bush's "standing confident" is not strength of character. It's more in character with stubborn idiocy, with a guy who does not know what the hell he's doing and covers up the fact by masquerading as a decisive, unbending figurehead who values a repeated, consistent message above facts and truth.

Autocratic leaders have always stood confident, in order to drum an incongruous message into their citizens' minds, and to discourage anyone from calling out the president's see-through clothes. You don't have to be a military guidance system machine-language programmer to see that American presence in Iraq is fueling the insurgency; that Iraq was without terrorists (and WMD!) before we broke down the borders; that we have stirred up world hatred by stirring up the hornet's nest of religious extremism.

Finally, it doesn't even take an Excel macro programmer to make the connection between the Bush/Cheney consortium and Big Industry. Remember the Faith Based Initiative? Funny how that sent lots of money to large Christian groups (led by the likes of Jerry Falwell) who of course vote heavily Republican. So why even entertain the possibility that a twenty-two percent increase in energy research isn't going to be anything more than another subsidy for Exxon or Texaco to pour into some black hole – or an oil CEO's retirement plan?

There were some real signs in the State of the Union address, all right. Signs that the Bush administration thinks we're pretty stupid. And why not? So far, We The People have proven to be.

N egative campaign advertisement or not, I do wish he had beat that challenger in the Republican primary:

CHAPTER 18

Joe Schwarz, Take II – January 6, 2006

Last September, I expressed my opinion that Joe Schwarz, our 7th District Representative, was "a Republican even I can like." As he strode past me during the Chelsea Fair parade, I had called out and asked him whether he would be protecting the Arctic National Wildlife Refuge, a vast stretch of pristine wilderness in Alaska, commonly referred to as the ANWR.

His response to me was as clear as a cardinal's call on a crisp, cold winter morning: "I will never vote for drilling in the Alaskan National Wildlife Refuge. Never."

On December 9, Representative Schwarz voted for House Rule (H.R.) 2863, which included a provision for drilling in the ANWR. This bill passed in the House.

Fortunately, the drilling provision was later stripped in the Senate. But this was much too close a call for me.

More importantly, it said something about a man's word. If you're going to say something, follow through with it. If you're not 100% certain you can follow through with it, don't say it.

I promptly sent an email to Representative Schwarz. I reminded him what he had said to me, and I told him I was disappointed. I immediately got a phone call from one of his aides, and we set up a time for a meeting. In the meantime, I did some research on the circumstances surrounding Schwarz's vote for ANWR drilling.

Representative Schwarz's rationale for voting in favor of this bill was that he had voted against an earlier rule (H.R. 639), which specifically placed ANWR into H.R. 2863. That rule had passed with bipartisan support, in spite of Mr. Schwarz's vote against it.

It reminds me of that memorable quote from the last presidential elections, which I'll dutifully paraphrase here: "I voted against it before I voted for it." That didn't fly in 2004, and it doesn't fly for me now.

In Schwarz's defense, there was some political maneuvering on both sides of the Congressional aisle. House Rule 2863 was a defense appropriations bill. It would have appeared "unpatriotic," I suppose, to vote against it, even if you were doing so on principle; for instance, to keep your word to your constituents. In Schwarz's words, it was "despicable to be put in a position of choosing between funding our troops and opposing bad public policy."

But if you're going to keep your word, you keep your word, and you explain later. There's not a congressman (nor citizen, I suspect) who doesn't support the troops, whether or not we support the invasion of Iraq. I'd give any one of the small handful of Congressmen who had to vote against a defense bill plenty of chance to explain themselves – they must have had strong reasons.

Last year I painted Joe Schwarz as a rare good, moderate Republican, not a neo-con like most these days. Not part of the Republican ring of corruption that's increasingly being exposed. (He had no ties to Jack Abramoff that I can find.)

Yet my support is wavering.

He has made numerous comments about supporting party leadership, which up until very recently meant Tom Delay; for example, from a press release: "As a member of the Republican Conference I have stood strong with House leadership on every procedural vote concerning the rules for consideration of legislation."

He recently sent me a disturbing piece of junk mail, a negative campaign ad targeted at his challenger for this year's election. I don't want to see a negative battle this year. I want Mr. Schwarz to stand up for what he believes in, to give me his word only when he's 100% certain he can follow it up, and to tell me exactly what he stands for. I want to be able to decide whether he's truly a

85

moderate Republican, one that would be good for everybody, or a neo-con just like the others.

I was compelled to write this letter to the editor in 2008, after Tim Walberg's two years in Congress:

This is the time of year that candidates pepper our mailboxes with campaign literature. They are required to label their literature so we know exactly who paid for it. For example, I received a postcard from Mark Schauer, candidate for 7th District U.S. Representative, labeled, "Paid for by Schauer for Congress."

Last week I received a whole-page campaign ad from incumbent Tim Walberg. The label said, "This mailing was prepared, published, and mailed at taxpayer expense." This shady character has also placed expensive, multiple-page inserts into several newspapers, all "published at taxpayer expense." That's your money, by the way.

He will claim that these were informational pieces, but we're not that stupid (although he and his campaign think we are). It's campaign time.

Walberg is part of the new Republican Party, which is happy to spend our money freely and ignore the cleanup, while claiming every other party is for "taxing and spending."

This guy has a history of similarly shady deals. In 2004 he unseated our effective, moderate Republican incumbent by claiming, "Joe Schwarz spent your money on trans-gendered street theater." In truth, the vote referenced by Walberg was on a 400-page bill called the Department of the Interior, Environment, and Related Agencies Appropriations Act of 2006. The bill funded veteran's health care, the National Institutes of Health, the Fish and Wildlife Service, our national parks, the Smithsonian Institution, and the Forest Service. There was but one paragraph funding the National Endowment for the Arts. The words "trans-gendered" or "street theater" never appeared in the bill. (Obviously the bill passed by a wide margin –

only eight Republicans were opposed – and the president promptly signed it into law.)

Walberg pursues a single-item, special interest agenda. He is the ultimate wolf-in-sheep's-clothing lurking in our Congress. Those who voted for him in 2006 should help fire him in 2008.

Mark Schauer truly works for the people of Michigan. He is passionate about us. And he's got a history of being above board and honest.

We should elect Mark Schauer in November for 7th District Representative.

After I wrote this next one, I concluded that it would be satisfying to craft an entire series of writings on the meanings of words we use to express our values – pride, patriotism, liberal, conservative, loyalty, bravery, commitment, justice, freedom, and so on.

The idea did not work well for "Other Voices." I preferred the freedom to be topical and to respond to current events or to scratch whatever writing itch I felt at the moment, be it blood donation, trail running, or fair elections.

The Pride piece will be a good place to start someday, down the road, if the project ever bubbles to the top of my list of ambitions.

CHAPTER 19

Values, Episode I, Pride – March 13, 2006

Pride. What does it mean?

As the mood of the country sours, as the president's approval rating heads over the cliff, as his Iraq invasion drags on and creates civil war, as the economy stalls, I ask myself, "What does it mean to say: I'm proud to be an American?"

Before you slap one of those Power of Pride bumper stickers on your pickup truck, you need to know what the word means. Merriam-Webster says that pride is "inordinate self-esteem or conceit" and "proud or disdainful behavior or treatment." The Oxford English Dictionary gives the first definition of pride as "satisfaction derived from one's own achievements...or from qualities or possessions that are widely admired." Which of your own achievements gives you the right to the Power of Pride in America?

Pride gets in the way when my wife and I argue. Neither of us is willing to give in, to admit to being wrong. It hurts our pride. How easily we forgot the "obey" part of "love, honor, and cherish." Giving in is a gesture that creates trust.

Pride is first on the list of things the Lord hates, if you read the Bible. (Proverbs.) "Pride goes before destruction, and a haughty spirit before a fall." Pride comes before a fall. America, are you listening? Look what pride did to Germany. Nations fall from within.

Humility is the opposite of pride. Every great religious leader has preached humility. Don't we pride ourselves on being a religious populace?

Pride as patriotism breeds an us-against-them attitude. It fosters the current wave of "they-ness" that makes us lump anyone who doesn't think the way we do into some group we can hate. At some point in your life, you come to a point where you either truly believe what you've been taught – that we're all sisters and brothers, all created equal – or not. If you do, then you're compelled to live your life accordingly. Or you become a hypocrite.

Patriotism is loved by monarchs and dictators, for it galvanizes the unsuspecting populace behind the tyrant. The unquestioning, witless masses are convinced to battle some undemonstrated threat, a threat created and defined by that same tyrant. Meanwhile, the harm he does to the country is accepted as collateral damage.

The dictionary also defines pride as "a reasonable or justifiable self-respect." Now there's a definition I can relate to, a justifiable feeling we each need to continue to earn. I have the right to feel proud if I accept the responsibility to work hard to positively influence others to act in a self-respecting way.

I can feel proud of America if our government is truly nurturing America's founding values, like: individual liberty, personal responsibility, courage, service, loyalty, lawfulness, and a Constitutionally-limited government.

But today, the government uses the ill-defined "terrorist threat" to limit our individual liberty and freedom. Our administration has made personal responsibility a joke. Courage? Forget it. Our leaders speak out until they get criticized, then they crawl back down into their holes.

We require service of our best and strongest people, in the prime of their lives, to support an invasion that's left thousands dead and tens of thousands wounded. And when they come home, we the people treat them like heroes, while the government disowns them.

Loyalty to America has been replaced with blind loyalty to a party, even if that party's platform shares nothing with our own personal values. Lawfulness has become "it ain't against the law if I don't get caught," or if I have a plausible excuse, true or not, a good lawyer, and a wad of money.

Finally, the greatest threat to our nation in its history is the loss of a Constitutionally-limited government. Historically, yes, we have had all three branches of government ruled by one party before. But none before this one has had the express goal of cementing power for themselves permanently. Texas representatives redrew districts to give Republicans a big increase in the House. The Senate Republicans are ready to use the "nuclear option" on the minority party. The Supreme Court is being loaded with conservative ideologues. The president wants special veto power to allow him to sign the conservative portions of a bill, while vetoing anything that doesn't fit the party line.

I am happy and lucky to live in America. I stand up for basic American values, and am fighting from the inside to keep America free and to keep it from turning into an aristocracy. I'm proud of our soldiers who are thrust into harm's way because they were promised an education or a chance to make some money, and those who believe they are fighting for our freedom. I'm proud of all our past soldiers who truly were.

But our government has me embarrassed to be an American. When I travel outside the U.S., frankly, I keep my mouth shut and my cowboy hat in my suitcase.

Before you write your letter, think long and hard about pride. What does it really mean to you? Do you live up to that standard?

Does America today?

On Thursday, April 13, 2006, Chelsea Reserve Officer Matthew Tuttle and Police Chief Scott Sumner were killed in a helicopter crash while assisting in a criminal pursuit. I used my column to reflect back on pride, and the way the word might apply to a situation like this.

CHAPTER 20

Values, Episode I, Pride, Revisited – April 17, 2006

A couple weeks ago I wrote about pride. I tried to dissect the word, to examine how it was defined, and to compare that definition to how we use it when we say it, write about it, or stick it on our bumpers next to the American flag.

What does it mean to be proud? Can we be proud of our deeds? Do our acts live up to an absolute moral standard (for example, most of the Ten Commandments work well both inside and outside the church)? Or do we hide pretentiously behind the word pride in order to justify unquestioning loyalty to outdated, selfish, and bigoted political and social evils like racism, sexism, greed, prejudice against the poor, or intolerance toward anyone too different from us?

This week it doesn't matter. We reserve the word pride for two men, Matt Tuttle and Scott Sumner.

My personal condolences go out to the families and friends of Matt and Scott, and to our whole community. Our loss is great.

Some would say they died honorably, serving their community and performing their duty. Some would say they died doing something they loved. But no one wants to die doing something they love; no one wants to die just for honor. We all want to live. If we must die, let it be well past age 100, quietly, in our sleep, satisfied we've lived a long and fruitful life, accomplished all our dreams, said goodbye to our children and spouses and friends, and left life's loose ends all tied up.

It's a tremendous travesty that Scott and Matt had their tender lives cut short. It's terribly unfair, and we have a right to be angry and sad for a while. We are incredibly proud of them and we will miss them a lot.

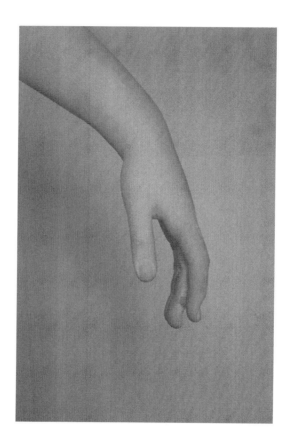

T he Tuttle/Sumner helicopter crash story unraveled slowly over the next couple weeks. Questions sprang forth, and answers emerged over a span of days. Why were the two in the helicopter? Why were they using Tuttle's private chopper? Why did the helicopter go down? Who was the suspect they were pursuing? What did he do? Was it worth the danger? Could the crime possibly have been worthy of the death of these two men?

Reasonable questions, the answer to which could come out over time, like they did when I was young, when reporters did footwork and interviews, and we picked up the newspaper each day or each week to find out what they had to report.

Things are different now. You know how I feel about Detroit news. "If it bleeds…."

CHAPTER 21

Men in Helicopters – April 24, 2006

If you were in town for the funerals last week, it was hard not to notice the news helicopters hovering over the Clock Tower and the cemetery. You couldn't help but pick up on the cruel irony of sending choppers out to a funeral for two beloved townsfolk who had died in a helicopter crash. The move was inconsiderate to the families (especially the children) and friends of Matt and Scott. It was disrespectful to the community. It was inexcusably tasteless and lazy considering the nature of the accident.

But I wasn't surprised. It fits right in with something I have been thinking about for a long time – the disturbing lack of depth, objectivity, and sensitivity we get from our major news outlets.

Serendipitously, an interesting report came out a month ago from the Project for Excellence in Journalism, a research institute affiliated with the Columbia University Graduate School of Journalism, and Heritage editor Michelle Rogers sent me a reminder on it. It confirms, as we are seeing, that we are experiencing a "new paradox of journalism," in which fewer news stories are being covered, the stories are shallower, and the stories are the same across multiple news outlets.

Let's take, for example, something like the Natalee Holloway case, which broke slowly, and was followed up by daily red-herring news events, each of which brought the case no closer to conclusion. [Natalee Holloway, an American student from Mountain Brook, Alabama, disappeared on May 30, 2005, at the end of a high school graduation trip to Aruba. Her disappearance caused a worldwide media sensation.]

As the story broke, and as the minor events happened each day, I hit the Web first. I use Yahoo. Invariably their news section listed reports from thirty different online newspapers. But they all used identical copy from the same story – either reprinting the *Associated Press* (AP) release or simply rewriting it a little.

On the nightly TV news, I got the same information, along with some unsatisfying video, after I waited through commercials and the misleading, "Coming up next, breaking news on the Natalee Holloway case!" There was never anything new, nothing breaking, and it was all the same across the three TV stations.

The next day I picked up USA Today and read, you guessed it, exactly the same information. And heard it in the news summaries on the radio.

Why?

In the words of this study, the public-service focus of the news industry is dying: "The decades-long battle at the top between idealists and accountants is now over. The idealists have lost." My guess is that it's cheaper to send a helicopter out to Chelsea – probably a three-hour job – than it is to drive out a van, which would take an entire day. It's all about money.

(Funny, so is politics these days. And the major media outlets are mixed up with Rupert Murdoch and the other rich ideologues, and the FCC is under the lobbyists' thumb…but let's not go down that road today.)

To increase profits, the networks have chosen to lay off reporters (in Philadelphia, the number has dropped from 500 to 220 since 1980), cut offerings (five AM radio stations carried news in Philly in 1980; now there are two), and rerun more content from other, often syndicated outlets. When your nightly news anchor announces, "In tonight's *Health and You* report, a surprising fact about locally-bottled water *that can kill you*," you can bet they are running a story that was purchased from a news service (for instance, the Cleveland Clinic News Service). These services assure the stories they sell have both a strong hook and the ability to be spun as local news. And they serve the interests of the greater entity (i.e., the Cleveland Clinic).

All this while three quarters of Americans believe the big news organizations are more concerned with attracting a big audience than informing the public, and believe that the media favors one side.

So it's only getting worse. The bean counters have won – and public has lost.

What does it mean to "inform the public" anyway? What purpose did the first three stories on Fox 2 News last night serve? A drive by shooting. A murder. A plane crash. "If it bleeds, it leads." Is that really relevant anymore? I wonder: if the Columbine disaster had gotten no press at all, would there be any copycats on the annual anniversary?

What can we do?

First, when you watch or listen to the news, ask yourself whether the anchor is trying to force you to feel one way or the other. I always feel like Monica Gayle and Carmen Harlan are trying to scare me, or thrill me, or urge me to sympathy. I just want the news, not the theatrics.

Second, do something about it! Write, call, and email your news outlets. Insist on the human touch. Tell them you are sick of hearing the bad news and being told to fear this or that. Tell them you want to hear the good news, the useful news. It's easy to search for their Website addresses and locate the Contact Us page.

Finally, we all need to become "sentinels" for one another, the report says. Full-time, professional monitoring of big news institutions is going away, and the news leaders are allowing it to happen, expecting it to be replaced by "citizen media" – blogs, for example. There is the potential for an expanding public forum, and a wider range of voices, but there will be no oversight. You will have to be very careful to take what Rush says, or what Savage says, or what Fox News says, or what ABC News Blog says, or what I say, with the appropriate grain of salt.

And if you don't like the way objective, sensitive news has become subjective and sensationalized; if you don't like getting the short shrift from your Michigan newspaper; if you feel disrespected by hovering helicopters because the Detroit TV stations didn't want to send out vans and reporters on foot, I only have this advice: speak up!

Or get used to it.

Or tune out?

In 2008, when Michelle Rogers was promoted, I was faced with battling her replacement, a radical right-wing guy from Detroit. I gave up, and quit publishing for a long time. As the wave of change in America was turned back in 2010, I was even more downhearted and unmotivated. But that can only last so long, and in the spring of 2011, I felt the urge to express myself reborn inside me. In the March 15 issue, the local *Sun Times News* printed a story about a homespun business, Souper Suzi's soups, and how she was shut down for not having the proper license for her business.

The following week, one irate citizen wrote to the newspaper about what a tragedy this was, and how it was all the fault of big government (whatever that honestly means) and overregulation. It only took one read of the letters page in the *Sun Times News* to get me started. I let my dinner go cold and penned a letter in response.

If one ideologue was going to veil his ideology behind an issue letter, I was going to reply, and not veil mine. I immediately regretted using such a radical voice, and at having failed with my use of what I thought was witty sarcasm.

I'll reprint the entire sequence here. It's quite fun!

(A note: In order to retrieve the text of Suzi's original letter, I braved calling her. She graciously offered to give me a printout, and I offered to drive up to Stockbridge to look her up. As I had hoped, Suzi is charming, sweet, and determined. She's got a darling farmhouse and a couple noisy cats. She's a motorcycle fan. I appreciated her Obama yard sign.

I bought three soups, and I ate them this week. Delicious!)

CHAPTER 22

Souper Suzi

All reprints by permission, *The Sun Times News*.

March 1, 2011 – Letter from Suzi Greenway, Stockbridge:
The beginning of the poem "Desiderata" says, "Go placidly amid the noise and haste and remember what peace there is in silence." It was always assumed to have been written by Anonymous.

It seems that Anonymous gets around, as he also lives in Stockbridge. And Anonymous does not seem to have read that poem, as he does not remember that there is peace in silence. Anonymous decided that my Souper Suzi's dream needed to be shattered and he called the Ingham County Dairy Board to complain about me.

I heard about this, and looked up the number in the phone book but there is not one listed. I guess you would have to be dealing with dairy products such as ice cream in a restaurant to know of this institution. In the end, it was channeled to the Department of Agriculture and they came to call on me today.

So I am sad to announce that as of today, Friday February 25, I can no longer sell my frozen soups, as I was in violation of the Cottage Industry Act in using cooked vegetables. I am sorry I can no longer serve the working people of Stockbridge with my delicious and nutritious soups that I loved to create and deliver with a smile.

I am facing dire circumstances in my private life, and this dream was going to help me survive. As of Tuesday March 1st, I will be giving away my freezer full of soup to anyone needing really good food created in this area. I probably will be selling the freezer too.

I am still allowed to bake my incredible breads, so at least "Breadzilla" lives.

In the end, we did find out that Max Erhmann wrote Desiderata, and I am sure we will learn who our local Anonymous is also. He obviously was not the one who wrote this lovely poem that I would love to share with you in its entirety.

"Go placidly amid the noise and haste
and remember what peace there is in silence.

As far as possible without surrender
be on good terms with all persons.
Speak your truth quietly and clearly;
and listen to others,
even the dull and the ignorant;
they too have their story.
Avoid loud and aggressive persons,
they are vexatious to the spirit.

If you compare yourself with others,
you may become vain or bitter;
for always there will be greater and lesser persons
than yourself.

Enjoy your achievements as well as your plans.
Keep interested in your own career, however humble;
it is a real possession in the changing fortunes of time.
Exercise caution in your business affairs;
for the world is full of trickery.
But let this not blind you to what virtue there is;
many persons strive for high ideals;
and everywhere life is full of heroism.

Be yourself.
Especially, do not feign affection.
Neither be cynical about love;
for in the face of all aridity and disenchantment

it is as perennial as the grass.

Take kindly the counsel of the years,
gracefully surrendering the things of youth.
Nurture strength of spirit to shield you
        in sudden misfortune.
But do not distress yourself with dark imaginings.
Many fears are born of fatigue and loneliness.

Beyond a wholesome discipline,
be gentle with yourself.
You are a child of the universe,
no less than the trees and the stars;
you have a right to be here.
And whether or not it is clear to you,
no doubt the universe is unfolding as it should.

Therefore be at peace with God,
whatever you conceive Him to be,
and whatever your labors and aspirations,
in the noisy confusion of life keep peace with your soul.

With all its sham, drudgery, and broken dreams,
it is still a beautiful world.
Be cheerful.
Strive to be happy."

March 8, 2011, Letter from Dan Zatkovich, Stockbridge: "Can't Overlook Safety"

I am writing in response to Suzi Greenway, who wrote in the March 1, 2011 edition that her Souper Suzi business — selling frozen soups out of her kitchen — was put out of business when an anonymous complainant alerted the Department of Agriculture, who found her business to violate health codes and shut it down. Ms. Greenway cites the Cottage Industry Act, which was put in place not to restrict *small food businesses, but to actually* exempt *a small business owner who produces and packages less than $15,000 per year of a 'non-potentially hazardous food.'*

Unfortunately for Ms. Greenway, her product was *a potentially hazardous food…I find it remarkable that Ms. Greenway thought it was her right to run a business that violated laws designed to protect the consumer from dangerous food-borne pathogens….*

March 8, 2011, Letter from Mark Bennett, Chelsea:
"If You Knew Suzi Like I Know Suzi"
I read with sadness the letter from Suzi about the attack on her home business by the State of Michigan. In a nutshell, that captured the nature of the Leviathan (a monstrous sea creature symbolizing evil in the Old Testament) that our government has become. Through the sanctimonious use of regulation, another budding business has been snuffed out in this state.

I don't know much about the specifics, but why is it that instead of her customers deciding if they like her soup, the state has made that decision for us? But that is the nature of the Leviathan. And in an insidious way (under the guise of protecting us) the Leviathan slowly has taken many of our rights away.

No one (except for Suzi and some of her customers) will miss the soup that could have been. But multiply what happened by 1,000 or 10,000. This is how opportunities are lost. People trying simply to make their life a little better by giving their customers what they want. Sometimes these businesses die, sometimes they survive, sometimes they thrive and end up employing many.

But if regulation strangles them, we are all worse off. We become more dependant (sic), rather than taking responsibility for ourselves to improve our life, our family and our community.

Let's take an example of how the Leviathan is not really interested in helping us. If I were to put an addition on my house so my grandchildren will have a place to sleep when they visit, several good things would happen in this community. I'd hire and pay a builder, the home values in my neighborhood might be enhanced, and I'd enjoy my home more. But offsetting those goods, my real estate taxes would probably increase.

Why should my taxes go up? The services the city, county, and state provide me haven't changed.

But as a result, I may decide not to build an addition, but instead buy a trailer and let the grandchildren sleep there when they visit. So a contractor and his employees don't get a contract (fewer jobs in the area). Home values in the neighborhood won't be enhanced, and I'll enjoy my property less. But my real estate taxes will stay the same.

That's just a hypothetical of the insidious nature of the Leviathan. Souper Suzi is a real life example that we all should mourn. And think of the thousands of businesses that don't get started. And think of the things that might have been.

The next day – the little birds flying around in my head:
- Thousands of businesses? Really?
- What happens when you raise the property values in your neighborhood? That's pretty much a universally good thing. But, contrary to the writer's point, when property values go up, real estate taxes go up. Everyone's. That's how the formula was designed to work.
- I have a hard time imagining being so bitter about a little tax increase that I'm unwilling to do something that I know will make my life better. And the life of my grandchildren, so they no longer have to sleep in the barn when they visit.
- "The services the city, county, and state provide me…." Seriously. How easily that rolls off the tongue. How quickly those services are taken for granted. If you're a true Libertarian, as this writer sounds, you should reject all government services. But seriously, we don't pay for services rendered on a piecemeal basis. We pay as a community for the sum of all services provided to our

community. We pay for ambulance and fire service so those services are there if we need them. Don't you pay any auto or health insurance?
- Finally, the free market is not, and has not been a viable solution since the time that the first small town became a city, and capitalism became greedism. It works well if there are two soup shops in a little town, and one makes better tasting soup. It does not work so well if that shop is also using MSG, salt, lard, chemicals, unsanitary practices, preservatives, and mystery meat, and spitting in your bowl. There is no way for the individual to sniff that out and migrate to the other shop. That's why communities band together to create rules governing those things, and create the infrastructure to allow those rules to be enforced. Oh, wait, that's called "evil government."
- I need to respond to this letter. But I need to keep it simple. Stupid.

March 15, 2011, Letter from me:
"This Is the Guy"

One hopes your readers are not as simple-minded as the argument of the letter writer who compared the government to the mythical Leviathan. He feels the Souper Suzi "tragedy" is an example of everything that's wrong with regulation.

This is the guy who forgets that regulations are put into place to protect citizens just like him.

This is the guy who would never buy Suzi's soup anyway, because soup is cheaper at Wal-Mart.

This is the guy who doesn't want to pay his fair share of real estate tax, nor any taxes for that matter.

This is the guy who rails against the government for not fixing the potholes and not having a policeman on every corner.

This is the guy who doesn't believe in paying for ambulance nor fire service because he has never used them.

This is the guy whose argument does not make the rational connection that government regulations are what prevent Wal-Mart from putting formaldehyde in the soup he buys and eats, and lying about it.

But that's the way arguments go these days – these guys take something they don't like, demonize it, and then use a one-dimensional, nonsensical argument to try to persuade the angry, uninformed masses to be afraid and act on their fears. At least the arguments made by those who kneel each night at the Fox News altar and offer prayers to their holy triumvirate of Glenn Beck, Bill O'Reilly, and Rupert Murdoch.

Upon further consideration:
OK, I was a bit out of line. This smacked of a personal attack. But I was incensed that the writer latched onto this issue, about which he "didn't know the specifics," as a cheap opportunity to express his neo-conservative beliefs. Why, I'd bet he could not have cared less about Suzi and her soup.

March 22, 2011, Letter from Anne Thomas, Stockbridge:
"Found Your Letter Typical of Liberals"

In reply to a letter to the Editor on 3-15-11, from the writer in Chelsea, I find your letter almost humorous and typical of liberals with low intelligence that attack the messenger, because he disagrees with their freedom to express opinions, which differ from his.

Now if he can only explain to all of us (or as he refers to us) simple minded citizens of Stockbridge, what Glenn Beck, Bill O'Reilly and Rupert Murdoch have to do with Souper Suzi without putting us to sleep, we can all settle back down to our continuing discussion on Souper Suzi.

Me thinks this writer lives in his own little liberal world, hooks on to any minor issue as an excuse to express his liberal beliefs, denying freedom of speech to others, and really could care less about Suzi.

One must remind the writer that Fox News is only ONE news channel, while his liberal news propaganda channels have FOUR. Big odds, as they say in Vegas, yet the Fox News he attacks somehow has become #1 in the nation to his bitter disappointment.

Now back to Souper Suzi!

Whew! That night – more little birds flying around in my head:

- By definition, "liberal" is a compliment, so thanks for applying the term to me so many times.
- Of course, any network but Fox is "liberal" – a political philosophy based on belief in progress (e.g., open mindedness and insight), the essential goodness of the human race, and the autonomy of the individual (i.e., freedom) and standing for the protection of political and civil liberties (i.e., rights).
- Since when is arguing equivalent to denying the other party freedom of speech?
- Someone missed the "triumvirate" reference to the big three neo-cons, and the tie-in with the Biblical reference to the Leviathan. But that was not a very classy move on my part. Friend Bob advised me strongly against writing my initial letter. It was not consistent with my fair and balanced voice from the past, he said.
- No need to respond here. It's like trying to explain Schrödinger's Cat to my chocolate lab.

March 22, 2011, Letter from Suzi Greenway, Stockbridge: "Out of the Struggles Come the Successes"

I would like to thank everyone who has replied to my letter regarding "Souper Suzi" either to me personally or to the Sun Times News, be it kind or unfavorably.

I would like to correct Mr. Zatkovich only in that the Anonymous tipster had not ever consumed my soup, and until Anonymous called the Ingham County Dairy Board which in turn sent notice to the MDA, I had not received one complaint from an actual customer.

The moment I learned I was in violation of the Cottage Industry Act by using cooked vegetables, I sent my letter to the paper to inform the public myself. I am very grateful for Barbara Malinoski's [a fine Chelsea liberal, friend of mine, and active member of the Western Washtenaw Democrats – Roy] *letter informing me and the public of the Chelsea Community Kitchen and I will be contacting her and other licensed kitchens in the area to restart "Souper Suzi."*

When this next part of my dream is realized, I will be able to sell my soup to the public again, not only through direct sales, but through restaurants and grocery stores. That was my goal in two years time, and now I will be able to get there sooner.

This experience has not been a defeat, but an earlier than expected victory.

Hooray! And I mean that. But wait, there's more...

March 29, 2011, Letter from Elsie Swanberg, Chelsea: "Thankful for Freedom"
Here's another writer from Chelsea who wishes to correct Anne Thomas regarding her letter to the Editor on 3/22/11.

First of all, the writer she wishes to condemn was referencing the previous writer (who incidentally was also from Chelsea) and did NOT refer to you or citizens of Stockbridge as 'simple minded.' [I did, in fact, carefully word the sentence in my letter. Have another look.]

And please explain how you feel he is denying freedom of speech to anyone, when your letter as well as his and mine are all accepted and available to everyone. That's Freedom of Speech. Let's be thankful we have it, and note too that Souper Suzi is back on the market largely because of Freedom of Speech.

And thanks to the Sun Times News for publishing both the positive and negative aspects of any problem.

Let the mudslinging begin:

April 5, 2011, Letter from Anne Thomas, Stockbridge: "Freedom of Speech Not Personal Attack"
I response to the letter from Elsie Swanberg of Chelsea, who feels compelled to justify the remarks from Mr. Schmidt, I make the following suggestions.

Freedom of speech does not give anyone the right to personal attacks, with remarks like "simple minded" that show an outright disregard for the other person. It does however allow you the freedom to express your own views on the issue, no more, no less. The original writer simply expressed their opinion on what they felt was an unjust attack on Souper Suzie (sic). Whether they were right or wrong again was not the issue, but the freedom to express their opinions was. While freedom of speech may allow you to use words indiscriminately such as, and I quote, "to those who kneel each night at the Fox News altar and offer prayers to their holy triumvirate" it should be clear to any moron, that some people might find it offensive, making a mockery of religious words they hold so dearly.

As to the rest of your response, it makes little difference if the person Mr. Schmidt referred to lives in Chelsea or Stockbridge, or the final outcome on Souper Suzi, as his attacks would bear the same result in any community.

With 85% of our students not meeting grade qualifications in this country, they will certainly need all the correct information they can get, not information some express simply because it meets their own false criteria.

Yep, no personal attacks in there....
And what did that final paragraph even mean?
Recap: I'm sure the editor was thrilled with the interest generated by the discussion. I started the thing, and then deftly

ducked out when it became simple mudslinging. And I have an unfair advantage by getting the last word in this book. That's the same thing I complained about when the last editor of the Chelsea Standard did it to me.

I have a hunch that all parties in the group could sit down together over drinks and get along just fine. Writing letters is impersonal and brings out the worst.

February 8, 2012, Article, Page 7, The Sun Times News:
"Entrepreneur Learns the Ropes of Michigan's New Cottage Industry Laws to Deliver Homemade Local Products"

Local chef and entrepreneur Suzi Greenway is back in business with "Souper Suzi" artisan soups.

After learning the business of cottage food industry in Michigan, Greenway met the requirements, became fully licensed and insured, and is making soup in a licensed kitchen to be delivered to hungry lunchtime workers throughout Stockbridge and Howell.

"Souper Suzi" features homemade soups in eight and twelve ounce frozen portions, and larger quantities upon request.

Headline soups include Broccoli Cheddar, Cauliflower and Cheddar, Corn Chowder, Asparagus, Sweet Potato Leek, Vegetable Beef Tomato Rice, and the unique Creamy Cauliflower Blue Cheese Bacon.

Greenway created a following with "Breadzilla," her home-baked breads that were featured throughout the summer at the Open Air Market of Stockbridge. She bakes and delivers White, Wheat, Cheese, Dill, Italian, Herbes de Provence, Scallion and Garlic, and Rosemary and Black Olive breads upon request.

A line of cooking sauces, "Saucy Suzi," is underway and will be available soon.

Deliveries of soup and bread are now available in the Stockbridge area on Tuesday and Friday and in Howell on Wednesday. Custom orders are available with twenty-four to forty-eight hours notice. Gift certificates are available. To order, call 517-851-7437.

Long story short: In 2004, some youthful, budding filmmakers shot a film inside our old farmhouse. They were nice; we became friends. We met up a few months later (9/25/2005) when director David Lynch, Dr. John Hagelin, and Dr. Fred Travis took the stage at the University of Michigan to speak on *Consciousness, Creativity, and the Brain*. My friends walked out shortly after they determined that Mr. Lynch's talk was not on filmmaking, but on Transcendental Meditation.

As part of his effort to promote meditation, his foundation was offering a handful of scholarships to learn TM. It's not free; it's not even cheap.

The scholarships were meant for students. I suppose the intent was to train people who were relatively young, so they could promote meditation as they moved from school and into the real world. I submitted my application anyway, and I was lucky to have been chosen by the foundation to receive one of the scholarships.

I was really only interested in meditation's stress-busting powers, but I was willing to jump in head first and become one of

TM's ambassadors. I became good friends with my teachers and fellow students, and, while I was still very active in the group, I received the invitation to visit the Maharishi University of Management (MUM) headquarters in Fairfield Iowa, and to meet my benefactor, Mr. David Lynch.

I was excited. I drove the 600 miles, keen not only on meeting Mr. Lynch, but also on getting away from work, meditating en masse, and hearing some interesting talks. In the end, my teacher arranged for me to dash up to Mr. Lynch after one of his talks, grab his hand, and quickly introduce myself. Dispelling any hint of awkwardness, Lynch looked me in the eye, warmly, and said to me, in his simple and genuine way, "You're going to do fine, just fine." Apparently that applied to everything I might ever do.

That was really all the conversation I needed, although I probably did not wash my hand the rest of that day.

I was plenty energized by the weekend, creatively stirred, and still pumped when I arrived home and submitted this column. Although my point was straightforward – that meditation in general is a good thing, and you would do well to try it – I did hear from a friend who had spent part of her life in Fairfield, and knew a more cultish side of the Maharishi Foundation, and wanted to share her perspective.

I was happy to hear it. Annabelle is one of several Facebook friends I have whose political or social leaning is quite different from mine, and yet we get along well, because we respect each other, and, when we discuss the issues, we express ourselves without getting into each other's faces. Annabelle knew I was not hooked, line and sinker, on TM. She wasn't warning or admonishing me. She also trusted that I would not take her message in the wrong way. She trusted that I would know where she was coming from.

These are the best kinds of friends – Republicans I don't know are Republicans, Christians I don't know are Christians, NRA members I don't know are NRA members, Bears fans I don't know are Bears fans, until some hint comes out by itself. Nothing in my face, no pressure, no persuasion, no arguments, no advertising, superior attitude, no attitude at all.

Free and open discourse with them is very fulfilling and satisfying. We listen to each other.

Anyway, here's what Annabelle said:

Hi Roy,

I had a close cousin who spent some time in Fairfield, Iowa when she was young, and I visited often. Living in Fairfield was, for the most part, a dream. Especially for parents. A lovely farming community, good schools, great town square, and at the time a fairly nice sized, albeit ill famed, four-year college. Indeed, the Parsons College campus was a lovely sprawling parcel of land with grand brick buildings and a lovely, historic chapel. Reputation be damned, it was a source of pride for Fairfield.

When the college fell into financial hardship, the campus was abandoned and stayed that way for some time. For how long, I don't remember. Then Maharishi International University expressed interest in the campus and the town.

The locals approached the idea of this type of university coming to their community with great trepidation. The community was very much split over the acceptance of MIU. But Iowans are an accepting lot and many starting meditating just to have a sense of what was to be. These were peaceful, earth-shoe wearing young students looking for a new approach to college. It would appear that though *a bit odd to the people of Fairfield, they were good people. Nothing to fear. In addition, the university folks pledged to become one with the community and embrace their new hometown. When the deals were finally made, MIU had become a reality in Fairfield.*

The changes to the town began slowly and subtly. Comments by the locals of the rudeness of the MIU students were frequent. Local merchants made little or no profit from the college since the student loyalty to the school and dietary concerns were dominant. MIU staff refused to hire locals for construction, landscaping, or other manual labor. The MIU faculty refused to send their kids to the public schools and the separation from the locals was clearly evident. Doug Henning came to town quite frequently and the Maharishi Mehesh Yogi made a few appearances, as well. The entire town rolled out the red carpet each time a dignitary came to town.

It wasn't long before the golden domes for "flying" went up. Fairfielders had gone from having a college that was a minor embarrassment in Parsons College to being humiliated and ashamed to admit where they were from as a result of MIU.

Pretty soon, thriving businesses around the square closed up and were sold to big money MIU residents. Today, when you walk around the square, you might see one or two original merchants. Otherwise, all stores are owned and operated by MIUers. Retail stores catering to the needs of the MIU community only!

What is even more disturbing is the new town developed north of Fairfield. MIU now contributes nothing to the tax base of the town of Fairfield. A town that accepted them so many years earlier, when other communities had refused.

On the other hand, a clean colon is a clean colon. Fairfield is now known for cleaning the colons of a number of famous celebrities.

Roy, this is more than just a sad "sour grapes" story. Nor is it a "good ole days" diatribe. What MIU did to our little town is unconscionable and I would caution you on your next visit. Because though you say they wanted nothing, proceed with caution my friend, things are not always as they appear.
   Annabelle

CHAPTER 23

The Odd Goings On in Fairfield, Iowa – March 27, 2006

I send this dispatch from Fairfield, Iowa. Let me tell you, it's flat out here. Spacious. And quiet. When I got up at six a.m. to run, the town dogs woke up with me. As I jogged across town, the dogs passed their message from neighborhood to neighborhood. "Here he comes! Bark, bark!" They cooperated in kind of a neural network of canines.

I'm here for a conference on physics, filmmaking, music, and creativity. And to meet some famous people, in particular a favorite filmmaker of mine.

I spent time with David Lynch, one of the great American film directors. His movies are striking. They are lush with texture and saturation. They are filled with troubling, dark images; acts of malevolence and evil; and moments of great beauty and peace. Lynch, this maker of dark, often violent films, is a gentle, candid man of extraordinary kindness, common sense, intelligence, and, mostly, inner peace.

I attended lectures by theoretical physicist John Hagelin, who has postulated a Grand Unified Field Theory, as Einstein predicted, that would describe the entire universe, including disparate forces like the strong and weak nuclear forces, magnetism, and gravity. Although I don't subscribe to all of his political ideas, I found Dr. Hagelin to be classically dry, academic, skeptical, and articulate. Above all, he is a man of extraordinary imagination, vision, optimism, hope, and, mostly, inner peace.

I enjoyed music from Donovan Leitch. Yes, that Donovan. The Hurdy Gurdy man who in 1967, along with George Harrison, rejected drugs for meditation. Still very popular in Europe, Donovan has released a dozen albums since his popularity peaked here in the U.S. It should not surprise you that Donovan is a man of inner peace, and his songs continue to reflect that.

Eight hundred attendees sat patiently, listened attentively, and applauded enthusiastically as Lynch, Hagelin, and Leitch spoke about such diverse topics as creativity and consciousness; quantum physics and superstring theory; brain wave synchrony during meditation (with a live demonstration); creating stress-free schools; treating ADHD without drugs; and most compelling to me, the science of peace.

Being a natural skeptic myself, I brought my conspiracy-theorist cloak along to the lectures. I kept wondering what was in this for them? Why take away a long weekend to speak to us on these topics? Lynch's time would be better spent at home working on his new movie (*Inland Empire*). Maybe Hagelin would be pushing his books, or the DVD version of his 2004 movie *What the #$*! Do We Know!?* Certainly Donovan would have a table in the lobby loaded down with signed copies of his new boxed set for sale, right? Or the conference hosts (the Maharishi University of Management) would be pushing Transcendental Meditation on all of us, at $2500 a pop. I was certain someone would eventually ask me for a donation, make me kneel and say "Jai Guru Dev," or pressure me to sign up for some sort of time share in Iowa.

But I didn't find it. No one was selling anything. I didn't even have to give up my email address or phone number.

The conference ended up being completely about these three great figures, three meditators, telling us how the simple habit of daily meditation has changed their lives, not only by reducing stress, but by incredibly enhancing their creativity, making their endeavors successful, and improving their focus and ability to think, come up with new ideas, and see them through to fruition. Their goal was only to help the rest of us, and to make us think about what's possible in this world – peace, personal satisfaction (ok, they call it "bliss"), cooperation among ourselves, enhanced spirituality within our own religions (and cooperation between them), and ultimately, peace through a reduction in aggression and violence worldwide.

Without becoming a cultist, without losing yourself to a political left or right ideology, without getting a PhD in physics, you can start now, simply by making a change within yourself. Pursue your own calmness, bliss, peace with your neighbors, emotional intimacy with your spouse, and prayer according to your beliefs. Feel free to consider learning to meditate.

If what I'm talking about is way too off the wall, then you have a problem. You have everything to gain by listening to and considering new ideas. To walk a mile in another's shoes does not mean you have to glue them to your feet.

David Lynch speaks with an amazing kindness, conviction, and candor. Compelling metaphors flow spontaneously from his mouth. During the free question period, a young man came forth from the large, conference hall crowd, approached one of the microphones, and asked Lynch what he thought about the polarization that people are feeling nowadays, about how political or religious discussions always become confrontations, and how all the parties are adversaries.

He answered that when a discussion turns, and starts to become an argument, we tend to become defensive. When someone wants to shoot down your ideas, you need to stop yourself, resist going on defense, and just listen. If you can't listen in the interest of understanding and being open minded, then just listen so you know what the other side is saying and you can file it away in memory, or use it some other time. Above all, make friends. Your influence is so much stronger when you become friends, instead of pushing the argument to its climax, and walking away enemies.

"We should all be like puppies, our tails wagging," he said.

I'd like to try that more often.

Over the months and years since that magical time in Fairfield, a bit of my enthusiasm has evaporated along with the memories. At the time, I was meditating twice a day, every day. It was Mr. Lynch's foundation that paid my fee into the official TM world. It bought me my secret mantra.

Nowadays I meditate only when I feel I need it, when life has closed in upon me and I no longer feel the open space of my existence, the earth, the universe. Not cool, I know. There is no doubt in my mind that meditation, when I maintained a decent practice once or twice a day, kept me about 100% healthier, emotionally, psychologically, spiritually, and even physically. But, like dieting, working out, or practicing Spanish, it's easy to skip one day...and the next...and the next...thinking I'll eventually find time to catch up.

I should get back to it. But there are so many shoulds.

I do know that after the conference, I was wildly creative, as Mr. Lynch had promised in his talk. (He later collected his thoughts into a wonderful book – *Catching the Big Fish* – to which I still refer, often.) I wrote a bucket full of songs and stories, many of them scribbled on scraps of paper during the long drive back to Michigan from Iowa.

With a conference like that, and a group like the Maharishi Foundation, you can definitely be pulled in in a cult-like sort of way. Or not! It's your choice. I was completely allowed to hang on the fringe during the conference. I experienced just one thread of an extensive fabric, and the TM folks had no problem with that. I reserve judgment on Hagelin's Unified Field Theory, on yogic flying, and on Vedic principles of architecture – although I would find a home built following those principles would be very pleasing and very beautiful, in the same way a space feels when it follows the principles of fung shui.

I have never been a person feeling a need, someone sensing something missing, some hole in my life. I have studied different religions because they are interesting. I attend church, albeit occasionally, because I want to. I have read about and thought about many philosophies because I enjoy being a lifelong student. I signed up for TM because I know there are stress-beating benefits of meditation. I admire the fact that there was never any pressure exerted upon me to become any more involved once I had completed my training. The only thing they asked was to please, please continue meditating on my own.

I should honor that, and maybe dig up and publish those songs and stories born in Iowa.

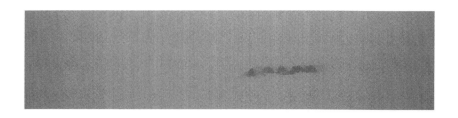

I have been mountaineering since I first moved from Wisconsin out to the state of Washington in 1989. I followed a compelling job offer at a manufacturing company that made equipment for the pulp and paper industry. It was my ticket to God's Country. One of my first work friends was Skip, the electrician. The first thing he did was pull me aside and teach me the right way to design a control panel, instead of the way I learned in college.

The second thing he did was tell me all about the great adventures waiting for me in God's Country. "You like the mountains? I guess you can ride a sled down the side of Mt. Hood."

Sledding? I thought. *Very cool.*

The next time I visited REI in Seattle, I picked up a brochure from Vertical Ventures or some similar outfit, and I called the number when I got home. "I heard you can sled down Mt. Hood. I'd like to find out about signing up for that."

Dead silence. Then, "Sledding?"

"Uh-huh."

"We can sign you up for a guided climb of Mt. Hood, but the only sledding is a bit of sliding on your butt on the way down."

"Oh. I see." I swallowed hard. Well. "I'll call back. No. Wait. Can you send me a schedule?"

A few days later I received price and date schedules, a description of the climb, and a list of equipment. For sure, no sled on the list, but there were plastic rain pants for glissading. Aha. I called and signed up, and the rest, as they say, is history.

During my years of climbing, I have formulated my attitudes and aspirations. For one, I prefer a good one-day climb. Rise at midnight, hike in the cool, crisp darkness, hit the summit between dawn and noon, and make it back to the car in time for dinner. Glissading optional but preferred. Multiple nights in a drafty tent, perched precariously on a glacier, with several other guys' sweaty socks hanging above my head, not so much.

But Denali, all eighteen days of it, was one climb I had to do. I'm working on all fifty state high points; I have always wanted to do one major climb; and Denali is the highest point on our continent, so there's that. I signed up for the climb in May 2006. Early in season. Colder than June, but safer; the crevasses are still frozen over.

Because of a series of exciting mishaps about which you will read in an eventual book, an eighteen-day climb stretched into a tedious twenty-three days. It was by far the most difficult thing I have ever done, not just keeping my sanity sitting idly for seven days while hordes of others made the summit, but managing the daily trudging, upward, carrying a pack and pulling a sled, 2000 feet at a time.

The experience taught me one of the most valuable lessons in my life: Sometimes there is no goal, long term, intermediate, or short term. There is just the monotonous trudging in the ultimate direction.

Sometimes you just have to keep going, without being able to depend on the certainty of an eventual summit, or the promise of a good night's rest and good meal at the next bivouac spot, or even the assurance of a rest stop when you really need it. I was at the whim of the mountain, the weather, and the pace set by the guides. There were times I could not take another step up Ski Hill, or Motorcycle Hill, or whatever hellish snowfield the guides were tramping up, and yet I had to, and so I did, before the rope attached to my waist pulled me over onto my face. No crutch was available to me – no urging myself to "just make it to the next rest stop" – because I didn't know when, or if, the next rest stop would come. I was beyond being helped by any crutch or mind trick. Determination and motivation were impossible to find. There was only the imperative: place one foot in front of the other. Again. Again. Again.

Since then, I have found that life is often like that.

CHAPTER 24

On Denali – June 19, 2006

I'm back!

I just spent twenty-three days in Alaska on the slopes of Denali. Some days it was fun. Some days I felt that whole-body-and-mind ecstasy that only comes when you are high on a glacier, trudging up a steep slope, sweating, aching, huffing and puffing, getting sunburned, but knowing that if you can just keep putting one foot in front of the other, you are going to stand on the summit.

Some days it was like a nightmare – damp, cold, blasted by wind, unable to sleep, tired of freeze dried meals, and wondering whether you were ever going to get home to your family, whom you missed dearly.

I learned some great lessons about patience, about tenacity, about discretion and valor, and about getting along with a diverse group of people, several of whom were packed into a tent with me and my stinky socks.

During the month I was away, I missed all of the Pistons' playoff games (will someone please tell me what the heck happened?). I missed the Tigers compiling the best record in baseball (no complaints – they're still winning). I missed the lilac bloom. I missed my son's birthday. I even missed both Free Comic Book Day and Free Fishing Day.

Upon my return, I had a few (hundred) emails to read. Three stood out. First was a nice letter from my friend Annabelle, in response to my column about meditation. I was happy to read her email and talk it over with her. We came to a neat understanding, and I learned from her.

Second was an email from a loyal reader, Elsie, who was nice enough to ask, "Where have you been? I keep looking for your comments in "Other Voices," and they have disappeared." That was kind.

Finally, there was a letter from someone who wanted to cancel his subscription because of my liberal, un-American, traitorous ramblings. I appreciated that letter as well.

I didn't agree with it, but that's the whole point. I have opinions, and it takes several hours to organize them and put them together into something readable. I don't get paid; in fact, because my real job is as an engineering consultant, I lose income while I'm writing these pieces. I do it because I can – the opinions page is there for me, and you, to use. It's part of the free speech we all enjoy.

The "Other Voices" forum is available to everyone. You can write too! Focus on something about which you are passionate. Argue with me. (Better yet, complain about Tim Skubick's insidious anti-Democrat editorials – that's why I originally started!)

Or write a letter to the editor. It's an incredibly quick, simple way to tear me apart. That's what free speech is all about – everyone getting a chance to talk, and everyone being willing to listen. If you don't like what you hear, don't close your ears. Listen! Digest it and come up with an opposing argument. That's not un-American, and neither is criticizing the government, the politicians, the invasion of Iraq, Guantanamo, the city council, the school board, the newspaper, or the cable company.

If we close our minds and our mouths, we'll never learn how similar we all are. In fact, we all have the same goals – we love America, we want what's best for all of us, we want peace and security, and in reality we get along well with most everyone we meet.

At 9,000 feet on Denali, I sat with Robert Taylor, a businessman from Texas. Robert runs a landscaping business, and he hires immigrant workers the right way – by traveling into Mexico, interviewing, and getting the proper work visas for his workers. We both agreed that immigrants already in the U.S. need a chance to earn their citizenship. We both agreed that the borders need to be controlled. I came to understand that his workers are real people, with real families and real aspirations, who have built their lives around their jobs.

Robert has adopted two kids from Russia. He gives his all to them. He is also part of a group that profiles kids for adoption, and he is now visiting a seventy-girl orphanage in Columbia for a week.

Robert and I talked politics at 11,000 feet, at 14,000 feet, and at 17,000 feet. In almost all cases, we saw eye to eye on ninety percent of what we discussed. We became close friends.

And yet Robert is a staunch conservative.

Interestingly, I can say the same about my dad, and about three out of four of my closest neighbors. All label themselves conservative, Republican. And me, a liberal in the midst of them. Yet we all see eye to eye on most of the current issues. We are all friends. We are kind to each other. We talk, often, about our opinions. And we listen to each other.

I'm sensing it's time for unity.

I n 2001, Consumer Reports named Stroh's beer the number one American Lager. Out of their sample, anyway.

Complex flavors, including light floral, fruity, dry-hop. Lighter body than most.

The brand is currently owned by Pabst Brewing Company, which has no actual breweries; the brewing is contracted out to Miller Brewing.

CHAPTER 25

On Campaign Signs and Beer Ads – July 10, 2006

I took a drive up to Brighton yesterday. I love that drive, up between Portage Lake and on through Pinckney. I see the campaign signs are out. They litter the lawns like empty beer cans after a Fourth of July picnic.

Some of those signs are huge. Vulgar. One could say that the candidate with the biggest signs was willing to spend the most money on that part of his or her campaign. The candidate with the biggest signs is going to garner the most name recognition. And the candidate with the greatest name recognition is going to get the most votes, especially among those of us who don't, or can't, take time to research every candidate in every race.

So, in the microcosm anyway, the big money leads to the win.

We are so busy these days, we either don't have time, or don't take time, to do the simple things we could do to make our individual lives a whole lot better. Like a little product research.

Last night I saw a beer commercial on TV. I'll give you two guesses what brand it was for. (Miller or Budweiser, of course.) In fact, it was for Bud Light. Bud Light completely typifies the state of marketing and politics (which are pretty much the same) right now. In reality, Bud Light is awful stuff. But it's probably the top selling beer in America. Why? Advertising. We're saturated with the brand, and when Aunt Petunia needs beer for her Fourth of July picnic, she doesn't know what else to reach for other than a case of Bud Light, which happens to be stacked on the first end cap in the store, and takes up the most space in the cooler, thanks to Anheuser Busch's marketing power.

Anheuser Busch rakes in billions of dollars a year. They are able to buy up advertising space all over radio, TV, newspapers, magazines, speedboats, stock cars, grocery store carts...need I go on? The American public, uninformed about whatever beer Anheuser Busch is pushing (in the free market, advertising comes first, and sales and consumption come after), will buy it because of the name recognition. And here's the rub: the old Libertarian/Conservative legend that the market will control itself – that is, if the beer is awful, the people will quit buying it and turn to something else – is a load of crap. If you're told often enough, and through enough media, that this is the beer to buy, you are going to buy it. Especially if the brand is able to use its money and power to push the other beers out of sight and out of mind.

It's pure human nature. If you see others drinking it, you're going to think there is something wrong with you if you don't like it. And of course you don't want to be seen as a flip-flopper either. Finally, loyalty is a virtue, right? "If you don't stand for something..."

Ultimately, if you drink it long enough, you will eventually develop a taste for it, and you'll think that it's what beer is supposed to taste like. In the end, Anheuser Busch has flooded with market with cheap, inferior product, and made you like it. They're laughing all the way to Ken Lay's after-funeral party.

Now back to local politics. You may not know anything about the guy with the big bucks (be it that judge up in Livingston county, the U. S. Representative from Jackson, or the rich big business owner from Grand Rapids) and the big signs, but you will remember seeing his or her name. And when you're looking at your ballot, and you don't recognize any of the contenders, because the others couldn't afford the advertising, it's just too dang easy to choose the Bud Light candidate.

Well, this fall it's going to be different. We have a major problem with money, politics, influence, and corruption right now, thanks mostly to the party of the super-rich. This fall we are going to vote for the candidates who are NOT ruled by money and greed. The huge campaign signs will be saying, "Don't vote for me!" We are going to go with the names on the smallest signs, or better yet the names that have no signs at all. And if we have time, we are going to do more candidate research in advance.

Will you join me? Let's get the little guy back into office, and get the fat cats out. Buy a microbrew porter with some flavor, or a Faygo cola. Vote for the write-in guy, not the guy with the money. We need to get big money out of politics, and it has to start immediately.

Stay tuned. Next I am going to tell you why Stroh's beer is actually one of the best tasting American lagers. Why to avoid Dick DeVos like the plague. And why to vote for Joe Schwarz in the primary, but not in the general election.

His Master's Voice

Why is it that we trust it simply because it's printed on paper? The media are not our masters.

CHAPTER 26

The Voice of the Mogul – July 17, 2006

I've noticed a new regular feature, the stealth editorial on the Commentary page, with the simple caption *Editorial*, and, conspicuously, no byline. Who writes these editorials? What are their credentials? Their position in the Heritage organization? Most of them are distinctly conservative in tone and philosophy, and I'm wondering if it's a conscious effort to drive the editorial page in a conservative direction.

The reader has the right to know.

The recent *Editorial* on the estate tax (July 13, 2006) presented the issue in a simplistic, and hence inaccurate way. It was short of hard facts and long on vague statements like "the [estate] tax...smacks of socialism."

By using the term "socialism," the author (who is...?) attempts to plant a distracting and upsetting image of Cold War Russia in our minds from the start. But the term socialism actually refers to a very wide array of social and political philosophies. It was first coined at the turn of the century in Western Europe, where critics were trying to repair the damage from years of inequality and excesses of poverty and during that time. Their goal was humanitarian, to create a fair and just system for all citizens, and thereby to reduce social unrest.

Oddly, bringing up the Soviet Union reminds us that it is individuals, and their pursuit of power, that ultimately mess up political systems – even a Democracy like ours – and one might even use the phrase "smacks of aristocracy" to describe the current White House and their base of "haves and have mores."

The editorial sustains the myth that without the external stimulus of money, people would not work to improve their lives. (Well, I did know a guy once who refused a pay raise because he would have to pay more child support. He was obviously an exception, and, I admit, not all that smart.) Let's face it; anyone intelligent who has a chance to improve their situation is going to take it.

Moreover, inheritance tax doesn't tax money that's in the process of being earned or spent, but merely the money the donor, upon death, gives away for anything non-charitable. In fact, passing your vast wealth on to your children disincentivizes them to work hard, much more so than income or capital gains taxes.

Think Paris Hilton's a hard worker? All that inheritance, all those parties, so few nights.

The author perpetuates another urban legend, that the rich "have more" (sounds nice, doesn't it?) because they either "worked for it, invested to earn it, or it was bequeathed to them." Wait a minute. Who gets rich digging ditches, holding down two jobs, working in a coal mine? Define ten very hard jobs (start with firefighter, teacher, farmer, trucker, auto mechanic, waitress), and then tell me if they make a guy rich. Compare one day's work for Bill Ford to one day's work on the assembly line down in the plant. Now compare their pay. Who's going to be able to "have more" with the money they made that day? Who does more golfing, traveling, shopping, investing?

Is it really fair to call investing money "earning?" Investing is not an honest day's work. It's more like gambling, without the house taking ninety-nine percent. You don't even need much luck to make a lot of money. And with that money, you can make more money. If I were that lucky, why shouldn't I pay some taxes on my good fortune, especially if it would fix some potholes in front of my house or feed some poor folks?

The apparent third type of rich person had their riches bequeathed to them. It was for these people that the estate tax was instituted. The purpose was to keep America from turning into an aristocracy like old Europe, where the rich could accumulate money and land, pass it on to their heirs, who could continue to accumulate more and more, effectively squeezing the middle class down into the lower class. The estate tax is a good vehicle for skimming off the fat of the rich and pumping it into the nation's needs, instead of skinning the middle class and poor. Historically, societies have broken down when unlimited inheritance has been allowed

With the fine art example (Anyone's wealthy parents collect fine art? Mine don't.) the writer of the editorial expresses compassion for those pitiful rich people, whose upper crust class is being singled out and penalized by the government. That's just not done in America – unless you're gay, African American, Hispanic, Muslim, or middle class.

One of the author's final points actually supports my position best – that of the Americans who died last year (2.5 million), only 1.17 percent left taxable estates. That's only 29,000 people out of a population of 300 million. This is a tiny number of people affected – and not family farmers, not small business owners, but the richest of the rich – for such a revenue benefit to our government. So why not actually expand the inheritance tax?

Don't fall for the age-old arguments, which aren't really true outside the abstract arena of idealism. Put simply, the super-rich want to keep their money. Wouldn't you? The rich run the government right now, so they are pushing for anything that helps them keep their money: income tax cuts, repeal of the estate tax, elimination of Social Security, reduction of benefits to the aged and needy, capital gains tax cuts, health care. But taxes are necessary to run a nation, and those taxes are not evil if they affect those who are lucky enough to have the substantially more money than the rest of us. That's not socialism. That's simply just and fair.

I n the ongoing pursuit of not getting cheated out of my summers. But more about that later.
For now, get up! Get out!

CHAPTER 27

Waterloo - Pinckney Hiking Trail – August 26, 2006

Last week I completed a personal goal: to run the Waterloo (western) portion of the Waterloo - Pinckney Hiking Trail from end to end. No, not all at once. It's about thirty-six miles long. I'll save that for some weekend when I have nothing better to do.

Meanwhile, I'll start on the Pinckney (eastern) portion. For now, it's a few miles at a time, often at a slow jog pace. I don't get a lot of fitness out of it, but I'm glad I do it.

Those few miles at a time are amazing. Every time I drag my sorry butt out of my cozy office chair, drive a couple miles to a trailhead, and plunge myself into the woods, I realize how essential it is to keep doing things that are outside of my routine. I'm reminded that it's such a tiny bit of inertia to overcome (simply GET UP!) in return for an incomparable experience.

Once I'm out there, it is, literally, otherworldly. Being out on the trail is completely different from my everyday world of teeth brushing, computing, cell-phoning, shopping for groceries, going to meetings or movies, watching the Tigers, and driving taxi for three kids.

It only takes about ten strides. I'm out of sight of the road, and in a forest so thick you might think you're out in the middle of the Amazon Rainforest, minus the hanging vines and macaws. I'm smack in the middle of what's left of the Great Lakes hardwood forest. The air is clean, with scents of fallen leaves, pine needles, humus soil. The trail bed is sandy in some spots, jumbled with softball-sized ankle-breakers in others. I'll scoot down through a tunnel of speckled alder, turn a corner, and come upon a hidden glade full of flowers and deer beds. No one tends this flowerbed, no one tills the soil in the spring, no one plants the flowers or sprays insecticide for pests. It just lives by itself, enjoyed by an endless progression of forest animals, but only by an occasional human passerby. Sometimes I just have to stop running, stand in awe, and take it all in.

Last run, I fought my way to the top of a short, steep, sandy hill to find myself looking out over a twenty-acre valley full of deer, monarch butterflies, and purple-topped milkweed. I paused my stopwatch, took a few welcome deep breaths. I turned to look behind me, and there, hidden and almost overgrown, was a huge, white cross, perhaps fifteen feet high. I hadn't seen it, head down, huffing up the slope. If you've been there, you know the place. If not, I challenge you to find it. It's out near the western end of the trail.

Before me a set of crumbling, wildweed encrusted railroad-tie steps led steeply down into the tangled depths of the valley. Warm air rose and brought to me a wave of apprehension. This place was wild. It looked like no one had been out here for a long, long time. And what about those rumors of cougars in Michigan? They have to eat something.

But down I went, again immersed in the wild. No candy wrappers or dog droppings. Not a question of meeting anyone on the trail. It was really no different, in my imaginative mind anyway, from my years back in the Pacific Northwest, out in the Olympics or on the Pacific Crest Trail.

I often wonder why I don't get out more often. I wonder what life would be like if I never bothered to spur myself off the same old track of life and into the unknown. I think I'd mold, mildew, or rot. Believe me, once you approach forty, the forces of mold, mildew, and rot become incredibly strong. At the same time, we become gradually weaker, nothing at all like we were when we were twenty-two years old. When we were invincible.

We need to fight the inertia of age, of glitzy toys and technology, of laziness, of empty overstimulation and distraction, of the daily grind. We need to get out!

Find a creek bed, a lakeshore, a wooded trail. Walk or sit quietly. The experience will reveal to you who you really are, the self that was buried and forgotten. It always reminds me that there is peace, at least in one small place, at one moment.

I'm not going to pretend that I'm fit, or that I'm disciplined, or that I'm better than anyone else because I get back to nature once a week. But I do know that it means everything to me, and if I didn't bother to do it, I'd never know what I was missing.

Move Forward! Healthy Choices for Kids and Families was an initiative of the Chelsea School District and Chelsea Community Hospital. This initiative was a comprehensive approach intended to produce lasting changes in dietary and physical behaviors of elementary students. The project involved elementary school students and their families at North Creek, Pierce Lake, and South Meadows Elementary Schools. The program was made possible by a grant from the Chelsea Community Foundation, which is part of the Community Foundation for Southeast Michigan.

What happened to it? Too much "government intrusion" into our rights, as parents, to allow our kids to be as unhealthy as they choose to be?

CHAPTER 28

Move Forward! – September 1, 2006

School has started again. Woo hoo!

I can now work a full eight hours a day, especially if I make my poor kids ride the bus to and from school. And I do, doggonit! The school bus is America's last dependable form of mass transportation. Now to get that idea of a car out of my sophomore's head.

"We'll see," is what I tell her.

My fourth grader couldn't sleep the night before the first day of school. He was too excited. The kid actually likes school. Well, let's face it, lots of kids do. Chelsea's got a great school system, and most of the teachers do a great job of kindling a fire of enthusiasm in the kids.

We pulled out my boy's brand new backpack and stuffed it full of supplies. Families were asked to provide a long list of extra classroom supplies this year, thanks to budget cuts, thanks to reduced tax revenues, thanks to the bad economy, thanks to spending $300 billion turning Iraq into a wasteland…yadda, yadda, yadda. (Please vote Democrat in November. Please?)

But I digress.

When it was time to pack the snack, I reached for the chocolate koala bears and a Hawaiian Punch.

"No!" my son exclaimed in panic. He's very sensitive these days, and there were almost tears in his eyes.

"What's the matter?" I asked him, getting down on one knee so we could see eye to eye.

"We can't bring those. We have to bring healthy food."

Hmm. What's this all about? Some subversive movement to force my child to eat well? Someone taking away his freedom of choice? Who's trying to force my kids to be healthy?

It's project Move Forward!, a partnership between the Chelsea School District and the Chelsea Community Hospital. It's subtitled, "Healthy choices for kids and families." The program engages third and fourth grade students in producing lasting positive changes in their dietary and physical behavior.

You mean my son doesn't have to fall into the same poor eating habits as I (and my dad) have, and grow up to have a nice round beer belly? I'm currently trying, for about the fiftieth time in twenty years, to get rid of it! If only I'd implanted good habits into my psyche in my early years.

I'm not going to explore the evils of society, the many bad influences against which we have to defend our kids. You already know about them: overeating of sugars, fats, and salt; too much TV, video, computer; super sizing by the fast food joints; not enough time riding bikes or running wild across town all day like we did when I was little and the streets were safe. But I am happy that this program is in place to help me defend my child.

As a matter of fact, without Move Forward!, I would have done nothing of the sort. And I'm not a lazy parent. My wife cooks great healthy meals, and we take good care of our kids, but it never crossed my mind to use the school day, the snacks I send, and the meals I buy (e.g., my child chooses) to teach my boy life lessons in staying healthy. The benefits of Move Forward! have trickled up to me.

Move Forward! makes healthy choices available on the lunch menu, encourages healthy snacks, limits treats and sweets during parties, regularly tests kids' body mass indices, educates our kids and has them journal their eating habits for a month, and communicates progress and findings with parents. By doing all these great things, they accomplish goals like instilling into our kids a lifelong interest in activity and fitness, changing the ratio of good food to bad that our kids take in, and promoting a grassroots kind of emphasis on healthful lifestyles that I hope will spread to the other schools, to other districts, and to the community.

For once, a program that tries to prevent problems before they happen. How much do we as a society spend on fixing things? Healthcare is a mess – burdened by diabetes, hypertension, and heart disease costs; taxpayers are burdened by costly crime enforcement, legal, and prison systems; our country is threatened by fanatical haters around the world. Imagine if we approached these problems by teaching our kids to eat and exercise; teaching each other sensible ethics and giving young, poor citizens options and opportunity; and being nice to the rest of the world.

How much we spend fixing lots of problems. How little we would need to spend to prevent them.

The latest orchestrated war-speak from Bush Administration officials, as they ramp up their oratory for the mid-term election, has recast Islamic militants and terrorists as "Islamic fascists." Thus, as we approach the five-year mark since terrorists attacked Americans on our own soil, the Administration is redefining the enemy - once again.

We have gone from the non sequitur of the "war on terrorism" (A war on "the use of violence and threats to intimidate or coerce for political purposes"?) to the neologism of the "war on Islamic fascists." Or, depending on the speaker, on "Islamofascism." Why the new rhetoric?

The answer is simple: Pure politics. Republicans, for good reason, are worried about losing control of Congress. (For less than rational reasons, many Americans believe Republicans are more effective than Democrats in fighting terrorists.) Should Republicans lose control of Congress, or either chamber, of course, it will mean the effective end of the Bush/Cheney presidency –

– John W. Dean, *Find Law,* September 9, 2006.

The Pentagon report on Friday said this: "Sectarian violence is spreading in Iraq and the security problems have become more complex than at any time since the U.S. invasion in 2003 ... Death squads and terrorists are locked in mutually reinforcing cycles of sectarian strife. ... The levels of violence are up and the sectarian quality of the violence is particularly acute and disturbing."

– Tim Russert, *2006 Meet the Press Senate Debate,* September 2006.

"Our commanders and diplomats on the ground believe that Iraq has not descended into a civil war."

– George W. Bush, *Weekly Radio Address,* September 2006.

The gang that brought you the "war on terror" is now prosecuting terror suspects at the same rate as they were before 9/11. So on the one hand, they're working their best to convince us that we have to be prepared to go after the bad guys, and on the other, they've bringing them in at a slower pace.

– Pre 9/11 Mentality - Terror Prosecution at Pre-9/11 Levels - Are We Safer?, *Daily Kos,* September 3, 2006.

... the White House released its updated plan for combating terrorism. The document describes many successes in the war on terrorism ... "America is safer, but we are not yet safe," the document concludes.

– Bush Warns Of Enduring Terror Threat, *Washington Post,* September 6, 2006.

And this, from a press release I found on *AmericaBlog*:
The ABC television network – a cog in the Walt Disney empire – unleashed a promotional blitz in the last week for a new "docudrama" called "The Path to 9/11." ABC bills the two-night production as a public service that is "based on the 9/11 Commission Report." That is false – it is actually a bald-faced conservative attempt to rewrite the history behind September 11th. The Walt Disney Corporation could have given Americans an honest look at September 11. Instead, the company abandoned its duty to the truth – and embraced the fiction known as "The Path to 9/11."

"The Path to 9/11" mocks the truth and dishonors the memory of 9/11 victims to serve a cheap, callous political agenda. It irresponsibly misrepresents the facts and completely distorts the truth. You should honor the trust the public has given you with our public airwaves by keeping this propaganda off the air.

"The Path to 9/11" attempts to slander Democrats right before Americans vote in a major election.

The miniseries, which was put together by right-wing conservative writers, relies on the old GOP playbook of using false threats of impending, ubiquitous acts of terrorism to scare Americans.

As Stan Lee would say, "Nuff said!"

CHAPTER 29

"The Path to 9/11" – September 8, 2006

WASHINGTON - Last week another damning piece of evidence came in. Not that we need any more; we haven't needed any for the last couple years. The Senate report on prewar intelligence on Iraq concluded there is no evidence Saddam Hussein had a relationship with Al-Qaida before 9/11.

Of course, the Democrats went up in a balloon. The report further undercuts President Bush's justification for going to war. But they've been up in that balloon fifty times now. When are they going to bring us back to Kansas!? This November, I hope, and you should too.

I'll say it one more time, and only one more time, so listen well. Read my lips. "THERE WAS NO CONNECTION BETWEEN IRAQ AND 9/11." And there is no connection between the invasion we are carrying out in Iraq and the so-called War on Terror.

What we really need is a War on Disinformation.

I honestly hope you did not take time to watch the fictional ABC drama over the weekend, "The Path to 9/11." The show was put together by right-wing writers, one of whom was confronted two weeks ago by 9/11 Commission member Richard Ben-Veniste after he watched the first half of the film. Among the inaccuracies:

Richard Clarke, the counterterrorism "czar" for the Clinton administration, described a key scene as "180 degrees from what happened." In the scene, a CIA field agent places a phone call to get the go ahead to kill Osama Bin Laden, then supposedly, actually *in his gun sights*, only to have senior White House administration officials refuse. Sandy Berger, President Clinton's National Security Advisor, called the scene "a total fabrication." Roger Cressey, a top Bush and Clinton counterterrorism official, said it was "something straight out of Disney and fantasyland. It's factually wrong. And that's shameful."

The former National Security Council head of counterterrorism says that President Clinton "approved every request made of him by the CIA and the U.S. military involving using force against bin Laden," and the 9/11 report says the CIA had full authority from President Clinton to strike Bin Laden. Yet the script, penned by Rush Limbaugh pal Cyrus Nowrasteh, claims President Clinton had "frequent opportunities in the '90s to stop Bin Laden in his tracks – but lacked the will to do so." A lie. Laughably.

ABC asked only the Republican co-chair of the 9/11 Commission to advise the makers of the film. The producers optioned two books, one written by a Bush appointee, as the basis of the screenplay – yet bill the miniseries as "based on the 9/11 Commission Report."

This was a conservative attempt to rewrite the history of 9/11 to blame Democrats, just in time for the election. ABC was trying to use the free airwaves to sell a slanderous, irresponsible fraud to the American people.

ABC has enlisted Scholastic, Inc. to send 100,000 letters to high school teachers, urging them to show students the movie. Scholastic has also created a discussion guide for teachers to use to encourage students and their families to watch this irresponsible fraud and then discuss it in school. The discussion guide does not in any way point out the concerns and criticisms that have been raised about the validity and accuracy of the film.

Here's a debate question: is it appropriate to ask someone to use examples from a docudrama to support assertions about actual events? A docudrama can help us imagine what might have happened in situations when we don't know what truly happened – such as *Flight 93* or *Richard III*. But the filmmakers assert that it is based on the 9/11 Commission report and yet make up situations that are not described there, and that people actually deny having happened.

Carol, a concerned parent of fourth and seventh graders in Chelsea, reviewed the Scholastic material and is ready to ask some questions of the school board.

"Can you imagine the tension felt by children with family in the armed services – who have no say in whether they fight or not? Children with parents who teach that war is wrong, children whose parents support the 'War on Terror,' or children with no discussion of this at home at all? Politics, just like religion, should be left out of the schools, especially with an electorate this divided. It puts children in a position to have to defend the beliefs, if any, taught at home. By opening this discussion, a teacher is forcing a family to bring this drivel into the living room. It may be cause for discussion in some houses, but it's just for ratings and profits, as far as ABC is concerned. Oh, and influencing voters in the upcoming election."

I hope you didn't watch it, and, if you did, your discussion focuses on how this was a movie, and not a documentary, and many parts were made up in order to influence people politically.

Do not fall for the fear tactics. Do not fall for the right-wing spin. We already made that mistake in 2000, and amazingly, again in 2004.

On 9/11 of 2007, the five-year anniversary of the World Trade Center bombings had passed a year before, and the ten-year anniversary was far down the road. The incident was slowly being forgotten, despite the inane "We Will Never Forget" slogan that those who are still bitter, those who in the end were beaten by the terrorists, have been trying to tie to its bumper along with a smattering of tin cans clamoring for more retaliation.

My mind was on nuclear power. I have always felt it's a pretty darn clean and decent way to produce power, especially when held up against fossil fuel burning or even gigantic bird-killing windmills. I was on my way to hear and meet Patrick Moore.

Note that his talk predated the Japan's Fukushima Daiichi nuclear disaster by about four years. I wonder whether he's doing the same presentation these days.

CHAPTER 30

Patrick Moore, Patrick Moore – September 23, 2007

On September 11, I dragged myself out of my cozy bed and drove to the Monroe County Community College for a breakfast speech, sponsored by the Monroe County Chamber of Commerce, titled *Meeting Our Future Energy Needs*. The speaker was Dr. Patrick Moore, former head of Greenpeace. I was excited on two counts – free breakfast, and a chance to meet the head of Greenpeace.

I copied the email invitation and forwarded it to my family and friends, subtly bragging about the bigwig with whom I would soon be swapping business cards, cell phone numbers, and tree-hugging tales.

When I got the chance, I read the invite more carefully. Aha: "founding member...former head..." speaking about the "important need for nuclear energy in Michigan and this country." Fine. Apparently I needed to do some heavy research before deciding whether to pedestal or demonize this guy. Google is always a fine place to start. From Wikipedia: "Patrick Moore, born 1947 in Winter Harbour, B.C., Canada, claims to be a founding member of Greenpeace, although he now criticizes the organization."

Reading further, Moore was in fact an early member of Greenpeace, and a member of the crew of the Phyllis Cormack – the chartered fishing boat that set out on the first Greenpeace voyage in 1971. Moore was on the 1975 expedition that confronted the Soviet whaling fleet, when a Soviet whaling boat fired a harpoon right over one of the Zodiac inflatables and into the back of a female sperm whale.

Oh, and Moore presided over and directed Greenpeace Canada and Greenpeace International for many years.

So Patrick Moore was legit enough as a founding member as far as I was concerned.

Now for the detractors. Paraphrasing Wikipedia, Moore has been criticized by environmentalists for some of his views, for having turned his back on the environmental movement, and for becoming a mouthpiece for some of the very interests Greenpeace was founded to counter. Moore has earned his living since the early 1990s primarily by consulting for, and publicly speaking to a wide variety of corporations and industry lobby groups.

That was a bit troubling to read, but you have to take Wikipedia with a grain of salt; its entries can be written and edited by anyone, including you and even me (gasp).

With research in my pocket, I was unbiased, open minded, and ready to meet Dr. Moore.

He spoke for half an hour in the plush auditorium at the college, acting as a spokesman for CASEnergy, the Clean and Safe Energy Coalition (a great example of Orwellian language if I ever heard one; didn't Bush and Cheney already use that for the coal industry?), which is a grassroots coalition of over 1200 members that unites unlikely allies across the business, environmental, academic, consumer, and labor communities to support nuclear energy.

Personally, throughout my years as a tree hugger, I always felt nuclear energy was maligned. The benefits seem to outweigh the risks by far. If you understand risk management, you know that you can't consider risk without considering probability. For example, riding in a car at seventy mph is incredibly risky (risks are possible outcomes, such as death or dismemberment)...but car accidents are extremely unlikely (probability defines likelihood). So we drive, despite the risks, because accidents are rare.

Thus it is with nuclear energy. A nuclear accident could be devastating. But what's the probability? Nuclear power advocates claim that there have been few civilian deaths (or none) due to nuclear plant accidents. There have only been two major nuclear power plant accidents in the last thirty years, and the after effects of these have been exaggerated. Nuclear waste is not the green glowing goo we see on The Simpsons. Storing it (not disposal – future technologies will allow us to extract the usable fuel, up to ninety percent of each rod, that remains) is like storing bricks encased in concrete. (Note: these statements are debatable. I'm no expert, and I don't claim to know all of the facts.)

In his thirty minutes, Dr. Patrick Moore didn't bash Greenpeace, nor dwell on why they are at odds with him. He did mention, offhand, that he feels Greenpeace is more a political activist movement than an environmental movement any more, and therefore less than effective.

Six billion people wake up each day on this planet with real needs for food, energy, and materials. To pretend that we are going to continue to (or begin to...?) meet those needs without expanding our sources of energy, and without utilizing technology, is to engage in pure fantasy, Moore said. Population growth, urbanization, global warming, hunger, energy crises are reality. Unstoppable. Do we wish them away? Or accept the inevitability and work within the new world order? Moore found he couldn't lead Greenpeace because he didn't subscribe to every one of their tenets – no nuclear power, no genetic engineering, zero population growth – despite the fact that he was (and still is) against killing whales and baby seals, H-bomb testing, and destruction of our environment. It would be like your church only accepting pro-choice, pro-military, isolationist gun owners as members. Because Greenpeace clings to their strict positions on a number of diverse issues, their membership will be naturally exclusive, and they will appear extreme. And these days, extremism doesn't work. It may help publicize their pet issues, but it also turns off eighty percent of the population.

Moore has deftly achieved the opposite – riding the Greenpeace train, despite having some differing views, in order to drive the Greenpeace train; and now riding with big industry to influence them to go his (green) way as well. The bulk of America is moderate; generally liberal. They're against abortion but in favor of choice; OK with hunting but in favor of limits on weapons; capitalistic but aware of the need for corporate oversight. Beyond us, at one extreme, lurk the NRA, Rupert Murdoch's media empire, the Religious Right, the right-to-lifers, the big industry lobbies. At the other extreme you have Earth First, eco-fascism, gun abolishment groups, and so on. None of these groups accurately represents any part of the majority of Americans. Rather, they endeavor to influence the majority of America from the fringes.

Fear is a major component of the tactics of both groups.

Right-wing extremists use fear to influence people. If we don't invade Iraq, if we give up cop killer bullets, if we tax the rich, if we provide health care to the poor, if we help the disadvantaged…the sky will fall. Be afraid. Be very afraid.

Left-wingers use fear as well. If we don't save the whales or the old-growth trees, if we don't protect our rights, if we don't address global warming, if we don't treat animals ethically… then very bad things will happen.

The difference is that the right-wingers don't necessarily believe what they want us to fear. They know we'll never really lose our gun rights; they know we won't turn into a welfare state; they just want to make sure no person gets help who doesn't deserve help, and that the big corporations and CEOs and already-rich folks protect their great wealth.

The Chicken Little left-wingers truly do live in fear. They really are afraid of global warming. They do love the trees and whales. They are afraid our Constitutional rights are being eroded as the government silences dissent. The problem is that sometimes they may be wrong, and without accepting and including these possibilities in their warnings, they come off as extreme. They become less than effective.

Dr. Patrick Moore appears to be one of us, the perfect mole to infiltrate the extremes and try to drag the players back into the mainstream. I may not agree with his views on logging and clear cutting, or whether global warming is actually good for the world, but I know his views are moderate. So are mine. We can converse with real civility.

And we did. Moore makes for enjoyable conversation. When he and I sat down together after his address, I did not prod him about Greenpeace, nor about nuclear power. I chose to ask him more personal questions. "Do we have a moral obligation to conserve and preserve portions of the environment for purely aesthetic value – like a species of whale, a stand of old growth, a mountain in Pennsylvania?"

"There is no absolute moral compass," Moore began. I'd quote him further but, not being a real reporter, all I can do is paraphrase: All we have is our own personal moral compass, and this compass changes and matures with time. The idea of enviro-moralism is fairly recent, within the last seventy-five years. Before the turn of the 19th century, it seemed natural resources were endless, infinite. No one questioned otherwise, until John Muir and others realized that we were becoming powerful enough to undermine our own resource base. He and others got us thinking about the need to care for our environment. This has affected our social moral compass, positively. At the same time, we tend to see natural landscapes in artistic terms, not ecological ones, and this has distorted our moral compass. A deer standing in a woody glade is pretty, but it can also represent food, crop destruction, species imbalance, and so on. We all need to honor the beauty of the scene as well as the utility of the resource depicted. We need to make our ecological decisions based on both concerns. We need to stay away from either extreme.

He brought his point home with a nuclear power example. Moore told me that nuclear power plants are often built within nature preserves. Seems oxymoronic. One might bristle at first about the despoiling of an artistic natural landscape by two man-made cooling towers. But do we consider the alternatives? More coal-burning plants, which pump poisons into the air that silently, invisibly despoil the same landscape?

Green technologies like wind or solar consume huge tracts of land, require construction on just as large a scale as with nuclear facilities, and kill plenty of (namely) birds in normal operation. I'm not against wind or solar, but the only green aspect of either seems to be that they are fossil fuel alternatives.

Personally, I would be happy to hike past a nuclear plant along, say, the Waterloo-Pinckney trail, or ride the bike paths around one, happy with the small footprint and virtual lack of pollution expelled. That's what my moral compass says.

Imagine if there were an absolute moral compass, one that would take personal opinion, attitude, and debate out of all equations. (Of course, we Christians have the Bible. But depending on how you interpret it, it either gives us complete dominion over the earth and license to plunder for our needs – or it requires us to honor and preserve the earth as God's beautiful creation. I'm not sure; the Bible fails as an absolute moral map; and what about the scared texts of the other world religions?) Would we be happy with the complete loss of freedom and free will?

What good does it do us, then, to be stuck with only subjective morals? Happily, it allows us to reach consensus, which would otherwise be impossible, considering human nature. Absolute moral rule would be like having only one of the two extremes – left or right – and no middle ground whatsoever. We would be at war with each other all the time, because only a few (pro-choice, pro-military, isolationist gun owners?) would be able to accept the absolute set of rules. With subjectivity, we can engage in meaningful debate, win each other over on a few points, and compromise on a solution that no one may be fully happy with, but everyone can live with. If only the extremists would keep out of the discussions, eh?

Moore flourishes in that middle ground, and detractors on both sides – big industry as well as the handful of environmental extremists, would do well to follow his lead. So would we.

I'm not saying corruption lives only on the right side of the aisle. Corruption lives wherever anyone with an agenda lives. I just believe a whole lot more lives on the right side of the aisle. Maybe it's just me.

CHAPTER 31

Absolute Power – October 9, 2006

If you'll pardon the cliché: All power tends to corrupt; absolute power corrupts absolutely.

In the Senate: Since 2001, Republican Senator George Allen has concealed from Congress the stock options he was receiving for his moonlighting as director of a high-tech company. He was also enlisting the Army to help a different business that was giving him stock.

In the House: Florida Republican Representative Mark Foley, who apparently has not come out of the closet yet (I can just imagine all those Florida rednecks who shook hands with him on the campaign trail desperately washing their hands now), has been engaging in inappropriate conduct with teenage boy pages, and for at least six years. One former male page says he had (adult) sex with Foley after receiving some of his explicit e-mails. At least three other Republican congressmen have known about Foley since 2000, and kept it quiet

In the White House: A congressional report shows a key aide to Karl Rove and President Bush had extensive contacts with Jack Abramoff – the Man Who Bought Washington – accepted gifts from him, and passed him inside White House information.

In Iraq: Of course, the Iraq invasion has lined the pockets of Cheney, Halliburton, and the Bush family. How about some of the others? Neil Livingstone, former Senate aide and State Department advisor, now heads GlobalOptions, a firm that provides contacts and consulting services to companies doing business in Iraq. Randy Scheunemann, a former Rumsfeld advisor who helped found the

Committee for the Liberation of Iraq, is now helping former Soviet states win business there. Margaret Bartel, who managed federal money channeled to the Iraqi National Congress, now heads a Washington consulting firm helping investors find Iraqi partners. Joe Allbaugh, who managed Bush's 2000 campaign (and later headed FEMA), and Edward Rogers, an aide to the first President Bush, recently helped set up two companies to promote business in postwar Iraq. Rogers' law firm has a $262,500 contract to represent Iraq's Kurdistan Democratic Party.

More Iraq: Vice President Cheney finally admitted that Iraq had nothing to do with 9/11. Yet he and President Bush have been telling us point blank all along that there was indisputable evidence of the connection. Even now, a huge chunk of the Fox-watching America continues to believe that Saddam was behind 9/11. Sadly, many of our service personnel in Iraq believe it too.

In the States: Forget the number of Republican governors who have accepted campaign contributions from Jack Abramoff. In Ohio, the Republican establishment is entangled in charges of improprieties in handling state pension funds. Ohio governor Bob Taft was convicted of ethics violations and misuse of state funds. Connecticut governor John Rowland is currently in prison. Indiana governor Mitch Daniels is under investigation for soliciting campaign donations in return for Indiana Department of Transportation contracts. Massachusetts governor Mitt Romney is involved in an ethics scandal for awarding a $10,000 contract to a conservative Boston Herald columnist to write columns supportive of Romney's policies. Vermont governor Jim Douglas opposed universal health care in Vermont while accepting huge contributions from the insurance industry. Spokane Washington Mayor Jim West apparently abused his office to obtain sexual favors and solicit sex over the Internet from underage males, and was recalled in 2005.

In Michigan: Representative Dave Camp was a recipient of contributions from Abramoff. Attorney General Mike Cox failed to pursue felony pollution charges against Graceland Fruit after a major

Department of Environmental Quality investigation. Representative Candice Miller was investigated by the House Ethics Committee for accepting campaign contributions in return for her vote on the 2004 Medicare bill.

Yes. Power corrupts. Absolute power, which the Republican Party has pursued since the disputed elections in 2000, and the fraudulent elections in 2004, corrupts absolutely.

Please get ready to vote against more corruption on November 7, 2006.

Please.

Koch Brothers Corruption…Right Here In River City…Under Our Noses…

– Peg Britton, *kansasprairie.net*, October 4, 2011

Cain's Campaign Tied To Corruption Of Koch Brothers

– *Blytheville (AR) Forum, via Associated Press*, October 16, 2011

Koch Brothers Elbow-Deep In Corruption And Murky Deals With Iran

– Michael Santo, *huliq.com*, October 23, 2011

Scott Walker, Wisconsin Governor, Eyed In Corruption Probe After FBI Raid On Cynthia Archer's Home

– Dinesh Ramde, *Huffington Post*, September 16, 2011

Expect More Arrests in Scott Walker Corruption Probe

– David Dayen, *firedoglake.com*, January 23, 2012

MJS [Milwaukee Journal Sentinel] Report Says Scott Walker is at the Heart of Criminal Corruption Probe

– Graeme Zielinski, *Green Bay Progressive*, May 29, 2012

Top [NY] Senate Republican Wrapped Up In Yonkers Corruption Trial

– Norman Oder/Laura Nahmias, *City & State/Manhattan Media*, March 6, 2012

P lease get ready to vote against more corruption on November 6, 2012. Please.

Cost of War to the United States, as of June 3, 2012, 9:33 p.m.:
Total Cost of Wars Since 2001: $1,338,812,859,371
Cost of Wars in Iraq: $804,108,688,372
Cost of Wars in Afghanistan: $534,704,170,998

Cost of War to the United States, as of June 10, 2012, 9:57 p.m.:
Total Cost of Wars Since 2001: $1,341,135,366,082
Cost of Wars in Iraq: $804,301,899,118
Cost of Wars in Afghanistan: $536,833,466,964

Cost of War to the United States, as of June 16, 2012, 3:15 p.m.:
Total Cost of Wars Since 2001: $1,343,028,751,365
Cost of Wars in Iraq: $804,459,410,992
Cost of Wars in Afghanistan: $538,569,340,373

– *costofwar.com*

CHAPTER 32

CANOPAS – January 15, 2007

I've been waiting to write about those CANOPAS people (Chelsea Area Network of Peace Activists and Supporters) since January, 2006. While jogging past the post office one Sunday I got this bright idea, an idea that had something to do with resolutions.

My resolutions for the year were to lose some pounds, to floss every morning, and to write more often. But think about the resolution, the resolve, of the CANOPAS people. They have been out there, rain, hail, sleet, or snow, every Sunday since January 1, 2003.

Public opinion back then supported the invasion of Iraq. There was even a group of pro-war demonstrators in Chelsea who set up katty-corner; they quickly dried up and blew away with the evaporating general public support for the invasion.

Public opinion is so fickle. It's saddening to think about how many Americans can't see beyond the spin, how many apparently don't use the God-given power of higher thinking. The peace-mongers knew back in 2002 that invading Iraq was wrong. Their level of support has not wavered. They were right back then, and they're still right now.

On Thursday night last week, the day after President Bush stubbornly announced his plans to send more troops, the CANOPAS people gathered in the cold. I couldn't help pulling over, parking, and walking up to see what these folks were all about.

They were all so nice. No Bush Bashing, no bad mouthing of Republicans, no mention of Rumsfeld, Cheney, Halliburton. And no political signs. Peace only.

Several of them were "Veterans for Peace."

Now for the big admission: They talked me into holding a sign for ten minutes.

I felt naked at first. Everyone driving by could see me! They would know exactly how I felt! But then I experienced the honks. The waves. The smiles. The thumbs ups. Anybody bitter just looked ahead, or turned away, or kept chatting on their cell phones. No middle fingers or rotten tomatoes.

And I learned something, big time. Before Thursday, I have to admit, I secretly wondered whether the CANOPAS folk might not "get a life" on Sunday from noon until one. Do you really need to express yourself for four straight years?

But while holding that sign, I realized just how many people these people touched: over the months, thousands of cars, thousands of people. I realized how many people saw us and were reminded: there is dissent out there, a lot of it.

F acebook! If you ain't on it, you don't know what yer missin'! Wink.

Roy Schmidt
Total Cost of Wars Since 2001: $1,330,117,657,393.

Imagine America's economy had we not wasted this money on needless wars that arguably accomplished nothing, and made us less safe.

Imagine a Republican president next year who starts spending another trillion on two more wars just as our recovery is gaining momentum.

You really want that?
Like · Comment · May 13 at 10:20pm ·

(Tom S, Char C, Deniz C and 32 others like this.)

Louis C: I don't think there is any president that could out spend your beloved Obama.

Anne S: Uh, W....

George B: With the $700 billion authorized by Congress in October 2008 (under Bush) via the Emergency Economic Stabilization Act, the Treasury Department has been doling out the money via an alphabet soup of different programs.

In July of 2010, the financial regulation overhaul reduced the amount authorized for TARP to $475 billion (under Obama).

Tim M: Since when is there a recovery and when did it start gaining momentum?

Bennett N: In case anyone cares, if Roy's figure is correct, it comes to more than $4400 for every man, woman and child presently living in the USA (given our estimated current pop. of 300M). Of course, that figure is higher if you factor it per household or per taxpayer.

Jim V: Wasted lives, and less importantly, wasted money on the wars could not have been accomplished without Democrats.

In the House, 215 Republicans voted Yes, 6 No and 2 Present; 81 Democrats voted Yes, 126 No (61% of the delegation) and 1 Present; the sole Independent voted No. The final vote was 296 Yes (69% of the House), 133 No, and 3 Present.

In the Senate, 28 Democrats voted Yes (56% of the delegation, including Senators Clinton, Kerry, Edwards, Biden, Bayh, and Daschle) and 22 voted No; 49 Republicans voted Yes and one voted No (Lincoln Chafee of Rhode Island). Note that the Democrats controlled the Senate and could have postponed a vote on the Resolution until after the November election.

And in 2007, Democrat controlled House AND Senate voted to continue financing the wars…including a vote of support from the current president. So really, these two new wars you are predicting, will have nothing to do with who is elected.

Roy S: I disagree. GWB and Dick Cheney led the charge to war. Without that charge, we would not have been in Iraq. Obama has pulled back from both Iraq and Afghanistan. Romney is talking about ramping up again for Iran. I'm just asking, are you ready to spend another trillion on a new war, right now? Yes or no is all I need.

Roy S: And furthermore, in 2001, the national debt Bush inherited was around $5.7T, give or take. Some of that debt in 2001 has to be attributed to Clinton, just as some of the debt in 2009 when Obama took office has to be attributed to Bush. When W. left office in 2009, the debt was nearly $11T. That's an increase of eighty-nine percent.

Under Obama (my fantasy gay lover, Lou!) [not that there's anything wrong with that!], the debt has increased from about $11T to about $15T, about forty percent.

Dustin S: No. We need to elect a Buddhist.

In 1999, Pam Byrnes (currently past Representative of the 52nd State House District) founded the Western Washtenaw Democratic Club over coffee at what was once Cousins Heritage Inn. Attendees of that initial meeting eagerly embraced Democratic political involvement in what was once an overwhelmingly Republican-dominated area of the county. Those individuals were ready to work in support of fellow Democrats seeking office throughout the western part of Washtenaw County.

Western Washtenaw County residents Pam Byrnes (Lyndon Township), Stephanie Pyne (Webster Township), Michael Williams (Sylvan Township), and Frank Grohnert (Lyndon Township) each took their turn as chairpersons during the earlier years of what is now known as the Western Washtenaw Democrats.

Since its earliest conception, the group has served as a vehicle for organizing and energizing Democrats in western Washtenaw County.

In less than ten years of existence, the Western Washtenaw Democrats have established remarkable success. As the population of the western section of Washtenaw County has developed, more individuals are now Democrats. In fact, in the 2004 election several former officers were elected to formal political positions. Those political successes were achieved, in part, due to strong membership support and efforts along the campaign trail.

– Abridged, *wwdems.org website*

CHAPTER 33

In Which Pooh Becomes Politically Involved – January 29, 2007

When the Democrats took over both houses of Congress last November, I decided it was time to get involved. We know the vices and downfalls of the Republican Party; we know what they have done to America over the last decade. Now the other party finally has a chance, and I want to help make sure they don't mess it up.

If you have read my "Other Voices" writings over the last couple years, thank you. You know that I have tried to be moderate. Middle of the road, common sense, with a focus on human morals. At the same time, hammering the regime in power, and hammering hard. If the Democrats follow the same sort of path, I'll hammer on them next.

If you're one of the vast majority of Americans who's moderate, you owe it to yourself and to your country to get involved too. Now is the time to find a group that supports your political views and go to a meeting or two, and submit your two cents.

Now, you know I am not talking about your anti-gun, anti-immigrant, anti-gay, anti-abortion groups. These organizations are neither liberal nor conservative. They are extreme. None of these issues, red herrings really, has ever created a job, made your life worse or better, or made a real difference. They never will.

I am talking about affiliating yourself with a group that has a platform, a club that finds and supports candidates who have a vision that includes the issues that really matter to you – and to everyone else – and not the extreme, fringe issues I started to list above.

In December I stumbled into a Western Washtenaw Democrats (WWD) meeting. I had been meaning to find out what this bunch is all about. And if I want to help steer things, I might as well get on board the train of the party that will be making the decisions.

Now for the good dirt. Last Thursday I became chairperson of that group. I'm proud of it, I'm excited, and I'm eager to move into 2007 and start changing this world for the better. One half county at a time.

But it's not for me to dictate America's direction, or even western Washtenaw County's. It's yours! Now is your chance to exercise your freedom to speak out, to shape the future.

I welcome you, warmly, to consider joining WWD. Come to the meetings and give your input! If you're not a joiner, attend our events and programs. We work hard to plan them and make them worthwhile. If you are a staunch member of another party, identify yourself, and engage us in civil discussion. Democrats are listeners.

You and I both want the best America, and the best Michigan, and the best Washtenaw County we can create. We can do it together, peacefully. Come to one of our events and influence our thinking.

VOTE ROY SCHMIDT, REPUBLICRAT FOR SYLVAN TOWNSHIP BOARD!

As of this writing, in the middle of 2012, I am actually running for political office. Well, you can barely call it that; it does not feel political, nor do I feel like a politician. It's more like trying to join a board of directors.

My township, Sylvan, is in deep trouble. We, along with the Washtenaw County Board of Commissioners, made some poor decisions years ago which are really hurting us now. Sylvan Township needs new, trustworthy, transparent leadership. Seeing as there are no aspiring politicians vying for the prestigious offices on the township board, a handful of us have decided to take matters into our own hands and form a slate.

We're a great mix – a liberal, a conservative, a libertarian, and an independent. In order to take on the incumbents at the first opportunity, we have registered our slate on the Republican primary ballot. It's not for personal or political gain (as opposed to the recent move by the real Roy Schmidt – who represents the 76th district, based in Grand Rapids, Michigan. He was first elected to the State House in 2008 as a Democrat and changed parties ten minutes before the 2012 filing deadline on May 15. He is currently under investigation by the Michigan State Police for potential voter fraud as a result of his last minute party change and the circumstances behind it.) but for the chance to serve the people of the township and give them the best chance to have fresh, competent, open-minded leadership that responds to the residents. We'll fix what we can of the broken mess.

VOTE ROY SCHMIDT, REPUBLICRAT FOR SYLVAN TOWNSHIP BOARD!

Thwarted by the new Heritage editor, I hadn't done much "Other Voices" writing in 2007. Once I had assumed leadership of the Western Washtenaw Democrats, I all but retired from submitting. I was confident I could still be taken seriously, but the editor of the Heritage chose to tack on my political title to my byline – and even to any simple letters to the editor I sent in. Full disclosure? Maybe. Making the most of an opportunity to spin me and what I wrote? Of course.

CHAPTER 34

Cesspool Jumping – June 27, 2008

In response to your *Guest Columnist* (actually a syndicated article) from June 19: A cesspool is a cesspool whether you try to call it a swimming pool or not.

If you search for supporting statistics, you can claim that this recession is not technically a recession. But look around. Everything at the grocery store is growing more and more expensive, from rice, to bread, to milk, to bananas. I pay higher health insurance premiums than ever, and now, as opposed to last year, I pay a deductible for literally everything – except maybe phone calls to the doctor's office. People are losing their pensions, losing retirement savings, losing homes, and losing jobs like crazy. The stock market is at a two-year low as I write this. And do I need to throw in gas prices?

Maybe Dan Calabrese is one of top five percent affluent in our country, those who aren't really affected by everyday living costs, those who accumulate more money trading Halliburton and Exxon stocks and speculating on oil prices than they do working their regular jobs, if they have them. But the readership of the *Chelsea Standard* is comprised of real people, who have to live in this world, day to day, and endure this recession/depression.

I won't accept lies, damn lies, or worst of all, statistics, even if they're thrust at me from a half-page "guest column." (In fact, "I have read" that seventy-six percent of all American journalists vote Republican, and sixty-nine percent of all news reporting in America is conservatively biased.)

Mr. Calabrese, and the management of this newspaper, can call my cesspool a swimming pool if they want to, but I choose not swim in it. They are, however, free to dive into their own.

M ore in the ongoing pursuit of not getting cheated out of my summers.
Walk!
Jog!
Run!
Bike!
Swim!
Fish!
Climb!
Garden!
You get the drill.

CHAPTER 35

Cheated! – July 9, 2009

I'm not going to get cheated out of my summer this year.

We had so many beautiful days last year. And I spent way too many of them holed up in my shadowy office, working, writing, or wasting my time on Facebook. When fall came, I honestly felt as though I had cheated myself out of my summer.

This spring I resolved not to allow it to happen again. I came up with a simple plan, a simple rule that was easy to remember: I would forcibly haul my butt out the door every time the weather was nice.

So far I have done a fine job. I've hardly missed a sunny day.

Even so, I still come face to face each morning with a steep, imposing psychological mountain to climb – and an inertial pull to stay at the bottom, inside my cave, rotting, idly catching up on email, uploading photos to Flickr, and only maybe doing actual billable work. I have to fight it every day.

Even though I am not on a formal fitness training program, I benefit doubly from a day outside and on my feet: it's another day not sitting at the computer eating M&Ms, and it's a day walking all those past M&Ms off my waistline.

Three years ago I set a personal goal for myself – to run the Waterloo-Pinckney Hiking Trail from end to end. At my age, running looks more like jogging, and end-to-end means a few miles a day spread over several weeks.

I accomplished my goal that year, and since then I hit the trail whenever I get the urge. (Someday, when I train for a marathon again, I will run the thirty-six miles all in a day. But I won't mention that here, because I don't want anyone to think I'm some kind of an iron man. If I can do it, this trail hiking and running can be done by anyone.) This year, I'm back to bagging short sections of the trail, stringing them together from the eastern terminus at Silver Lake to the western end at Portage Lake. As of this writing, I'm about two-thirds done.

Initially, I was surprised to learn that the trailheads are right outside my back door – within a few miles. I had been to Silver Lake before; I had driven past Portage Lake. There are plenty of other trailheads, any of them a short drive from Dexter or Chelsea. As a runner, I find the dirt, rocks, and rolling hills make exercise a heck of a lot more interesting than the same old round-the-country-block four-mile loop.

Silver Lake has that wonderful beach, so it's a nice place to start and end a hike. Depending on your route (the trailheads are segregated now), you may cross paths with mountain bikers. I'm firmly of the opinion that we can share the trails. I've never had any cyclists throw water bottles at me; the bikers I meet are always nice, if not a little preoccupied with trying to avoid running me over or going head-over-heels off the narrow trail. I find it wisest to step well off the trail and give them plenty of room. I'm always up for a rest.

On the other terminus, near Portage Lake, you'll meet horses. I find that perfectly charming. I give them an even wider berth, as you can imagine. No worries; you can hear them coming well in advance. And no, I do not lug my iPod along. There is music in the bird songs, the wind in the trees, the distant brook.

On the many miles of trails between the two lakes, I enjoy plenty of solitude. Honestly, I can count on one hand the number of folks I have met on the trails outside of the five miles at either end. Instead, I get real wilderness, like the large animal (small elephant or musk ox were my first thoughts), hidden by thick brush, startled by me, crashing and splashing into the swamp last week.

Every time I drag myself out for a trail run or a short hike, I see something surprising, amazing, satisfying. Last year, it was a snapping turtle the size of a garbage can lid, suspended in the water below the footbridge across Pickerel Lake, glaring up at me.

Near Blind Lake, off the trail, there are anthills the size of VW Beetles. It's the stuff of my wife's nightmares. Yet each one is mesmerizing in its beauty. I learned that it was a bad idea to walk up to one, stand there, and gaze at the stunning way it shimmers with the activity of a million tiny creatures. They were also underfoot, and onto my shoes, and up my legs. Thank goodness they were not biting ants.

Further down the trail there are little wild blackberries. (Yes, ripe right now.) I was making great time until I found them.

Where the trail crosses beneath the big transmission line near Hadley Road, you can look east and see for miles across green, wavy fields of lush grass. You can look west over acres of corn and big old red barns.

Toward the Waterloo end, nearer to Clear Lake Road, there are hidden ponds, covered with lime green algae, that glow like emeralds when the sunbeams cut through the foliage.

Time spent is guilt free on my trail visits. My mental health has improved wonderfully. My sons are old enough to come along with me, so we're bonding. And with the current economy, I have less of that billable work to keep me rotting in the office. So I'm good. But I think I would be anyway: the more we work, the more money we make, but, perhaps, the less we live. I'm choosing to live more.

Enjoying the outdoors in this way is a cost-free activity – and that's important to me these days. You might think the kids won't be able to stand being away from TV, video games, and Twitter. But mine have been enthralled by what they have encountered in the woods. For them – a bit apprehensive about the outdoors – the local trails have provided a non-intimidating introduction. They appreciate the vistas and views, embracing the opportunity to explore and set their imaginations free. And they get to eat the wild berries.

Each day, each week, each month seems to slip away so silently, years disappearing, moments passing me by unnoticed. I need to snatch them when I can. So I have to go now. It's sunny and seventy-five. It's time to grab hold of my summer.

Some rules of the road: Bring a little water. Bring a pocket camera. Share the trail. Don't rush. Have fun! There are maps posted at trail intersections. For more information and to get the classic map, just search the Web for "Waterloo-Pinckney Hiking Trail," call the headquarters, or stop at a Michigan DNR office.

A tragic accident took place in late summer 2011, just days before the first week of the new school year. It hit very close to home for me.

Writing has always served as a cathartic emotional release. When life weighs too heavily on my mind, I write. It helps. It purges the demons. I had not written seriously in a long time, but after what happened that summer, I needed to write.

It's not a good idea to write about something emotional while you are in the middle of it. Sometimes it takes a couple years to come to grips with a traumatic incident. But I wasn't intending to create art; I just needed to vent. As it turned out, the resulting writing serves well as a final story for this book, a matching bookend to the first chapter, Unity, and I won't apologize for the highly personal, emotional nature of it, nor for the ultimate tone of despair.

In fact, I'm comfortable with how emotional I can be, with how I can wallow in uncontrolled compassion, with how I can idealistically hope for a world without so much pain, suffering, fighting, and unhappiness. I suppose I fit neatly into the Bleeding

Heart Liberal stereotype. But honestly, shame on anyone who doesn't, because these are the hardhearted. These are the greedy and selfish and judgmental. These are the takers, not the givers. These are the religious hypocrites. These are the people who make our world a worse place to live.

Blessed are the bleeding hearts.

CHAPTER 36

Another Kind of Unity – September 3, 2011

At 6:00 a.m. on a very dark Friday morning, September 2, 2011, my fourteen-year-old son Roy crawled out of the passenger seat of my car. He said a groggy goodbye and melted into the blackness of the Chelsea High School parking lot, disappearing among the silhouettes of his cross country teammates milling and stretching under a security lamp, all waiting to start the first early morning training run of their new season.

At 7:30 a.m. I sat in my office, the windows still dark, my computer monitor glowing, the fluorescent lights buzzing quietly overhead. My cell phone rattled on the hard desk. There was a text message from Roy: *"Just saying in case you heard anything I'm fine."*

The skin on the back of my neck tightened. I sat up in my chair. *"Huh? Please explain,"* I texted back. No reply. I re-sent it. Still nothing, even after ten minutes.

On my monitor, an email popped into my inbox. There was a message from the Chelsea Police Department (via the Nixle service), no less cryptic: *"Freer Rd is closed until further notice."*

The prospect of a productive day faded like the morning darkness outside my window.

Something bad had happened. I had no idea what it was, but I had a sick feeling it was big. My son was apparently safe, but that thought didn't really give me comfort.

I called my friend Margaret, whose son Jack runs with Roy on the team. "I haven't heard anything at all," she said. "Let me call around and see what I can find out."

Twenty tense minutes later, a message from Margaret: *"It was Kersch, he's in the hospital, and may be really bad."*

I slumped. In the minutes between calls and messages and emails, I had convinced myself that whatever accident had happened was likely minor, that at worst it had startled the kids and maybe interrupted their practice.

I closed the priority list I had been working on, gathered my papers and put them back into their folders, and packed my briefcase.

Kersch Ray was thirteen, a friend of Roy's. They were freshmen, new to the high school cross country team, and both in about the same shape. They had run most of the recent training runs side by side. They had shared many of the same teachers since kindergarten.

I met Kersch six years before, when he was in the third grade. I enjoyed dropping in once a week to help some of the students with their in-class work. I took the liberty of picking out the kids who, in my very subjective judgment, were having a hard time focusing their attention. Kersch was a likeable, friendly, engaging boy with intense eyes and a head of lush, bright blond hair. He did decent work when he was not turned around in his seat talking to Tanner or Michael or one of the girls. Kersch, I decided, would be my project.

Over the next few weeks, I tried to tuck him under my proverbial wing. But that's hard to do when you visit the class only once or twice a week. I did my best to impart big-brotherly wisdom about the importance of doing well in school and putting your best into your schoolwork. I tried to teach him to focus. Like any third grader, he picked up a little, but I am sure most of my lessons were forgotten as quickly as my own kids forget that they are always expected to put away their dishes after dinner.

In the same way, I think that fewer than a handful of the kids remembered me or the other parent-tutors once the school year ended, not like we remembered them, and still do.

Once I received Margaret's message, and absorbed the news about Kersch, I quickly expressed myself online:

"To Our Kids: There are scores of adults, teachers, brothers and sisters, older kids, and community folks who know who you are from school events or activities or sports, from seeing your picture in the newspaper when you were going into kindergarten or participating in the fair or graduating from high school, from knowing your parents, and so on. There's this huge circle of people who all care about you, and you don't even know it. When something happens to you, good or bad, it affects a lot of people. It touches their hearts and souls. There's lots of praying going on in Chelsea right now for one kid."

I spent the remainder of my day trying to reach my son, trying to gather information from other parents, watching my email, my cell phone, my Facebook account. Once I understood the extent of Kersch's injuries, the broken legs, the closed head injury, the critical condition, I was spent. I asked my boss if I could head home, and embarrassed myself by choking back tears.

When I finally found my son, he kept telling me he was "fine," but at the same time, told me he could not get the images out of his head. When the tires had screeched, everyone turned, and witnessed Kersch being hit, taking flight, landing in a bent, broken, unnatural heap. The crumpled body. The coach breathing life back into him. The distraught driver. The ambulance lights flashing in the predawn twilight.

No, my son was not fine.

Nor am I. I've been secretly, quietly shedding tears ever since the accident. Every time I feel my eyes well with tears, I wander away from my family and into my office or out to the back yard.

There are stages of grief; there is a spectrum of feelings that come with trauma like this.

Depression and sadness – so many thoughts running around in my head. *Why did this happen? How can I turn back the clock? How will Kersch's family ever cope with such a tragedy? How about Coach? How about the driver?* Any one of the people involved could have rolled out of bed thirty seconds later, and this would not have happened. How can that possibly be fair?

Anger – at the driver, at Coach, at the person who programmed the stoplights at Old 12 and Freer, at the team for not bunching up. So much anger directed at the wrong people, because I knew nothing of the real details. As the weekend rolled on, I realized there was no one at whom to be angry. Literally, no one had done wrong. No one was at fault. There's a victim, but no villain. Oddly frustrating.

Curiously, I felt the most anger at others, people unrelated to the incident, innocent people I judge harshly. Funny how those people are the ones who exhibit the same vices that I do, only worse. People who are grossly out of shape. People who are addicted. People who drink too much. People who are grouchy. *Why couldn't this have happened to one of them instead?* I asked aloud as I drove home, slamming the steering wheel and pointing at some low-life person, in my holy judgment, waddling up the sidewalk.

Finally, guilt – irrational, but normal. *Why did Kersch deserve this more than I or someone else? Why were my son and all the others spared? Why didn't I volunteer to run with the team? Why haven't we thought about outfitting them all with reflective vests? What right do I have to be happy, when the Rays have possibly received a life sentence of pain?*

There are no answers, and, as I write this, the Rays are still hoping Kersch can learn to walk and talk again. The best I can do is engage in emotional self-preservation – quit worrying, being sad, feeling nauseous, and losing sleep. There are so man others taking care of those things; they don't need me.

And, I guess, pray to a god in whom I no longer have faith.

Six years and four months ago, I wrote my first real "Other Voices" editorial. It is eerily, unsettlingly similar.

For what do I search? Unity? In 2005, I saw it in my church, I saw it in my community, and I saw it through my local newspaper.

In 2011, I see it in the team and community, on a big painted rock, and online. Early Saturday, the day after the incident, a new page sprung up, *Prayers for Kersch*. I clicked the link to support the page, and became the 573rd friend. By the time I was done reading some of the posts, the page had over 600 friends. The next morning, 1200. As of this writing, over 3000.

Whether you believe in prayer, or in the power of collective thought and love and best wishes sent, we have a whole community pulling for Kersch whom, his incredibly upbeat, positive, faithful mother unfailingly reports, is "on the mend." I've spent the last five years trying to convince people that we need this kind of unity in order to solve our political problems. But today, as in May 2005, I think we need this unity simply to help ourselves cope.

The first time I visited Kersch in the hospital, I held his limp hand and put my face close to his bandaged head and whispered that everyone was thinking about him and praying for him, and that I knew he was in there, and not to be afraid.

After a few days, his mother Jackie seemed more deeply worried than she had been at the beginning, when the only worry was whether Kersch would survive. Now he was still asleep. The conversations in the room were charged with tension. We all wanted him to wake up right away. We wanted him to relieve us and make us feel better. I wondered if our unintentional selfishness was placing an additional burden on Kersch. I crouched again by his ear and said, "Hey, it's me again, Roy's dad. I know you're in there. I know you can hear me. A lot of people want you to wake up. But don't be in a hurry. Just rest and heal. We can all wait until you are ready."

Within two weeks of my first visit, Kersch did stir. I guess we all thought he would open his eyes and sing out, "Happy Birthday!" like Frosty the Snowman, but he was more like a newborn baby. He couldn't even smile back at us. I had a hard time visiting then, because I was afraid that now that he was awake, the healing process was finished. I imagined him spending the rest of his life on the edge of the comatose darkness from which he had just emerged. I could hold his hand, but I was so close to tears I couldn't say anything. I was afraid my feelings were carrying negativity to him. I tried to send positive thoughts.

On the way home, I told God that he could give me all the pulled muscles, sprains, tendinitis, cramps, plantar fasciitis, backaches, and black toes he wanted, as long as whatever health he took away from me, he gave to Kersch. I have enjoyed had my share of all of those ailments as part of my marathon training. Meanwhile,

Kersch made excruciatingly slow, but incrementally positive progress, until he was able to interact with Jackie and others close to him.

I made it a habit to always sit at the same side of the bed, hold his hand, and introduce myself as the father of his friend, my son. Each time, his hands felt warmer, his grip grew stronger, and more life coursed through his fingers. Now I didn't bend to his ear, I just talked, and said I was proud of him, and told him that he was still free to take his own sweet time. Quietly, privately, I apologized for the way most of us were talking to him, patronizingly, like he was a baby.

I visited him again when he was more alert, sitting up in his wheelchair, but still unable to talk, still worrisomely crippled. If the real Kersch really was "inside," was he destined to be something like Jean-Dominique Bauby, imprisoned inside a feeble body, communicating with winks and grunts? I patronizingly introduced myself again, and said it was nice to see him, and that he was looking better.

But this time, when I took his hand, he held it for just a beat, about as long as you would take to shake another man's hand. Then, as I tried to hold it longer, like I would hold a toddler's hand, he let go. He actually pushed my hand away.

And in that moment, I was filled with joy and relief. If you know Kersch, you know he's not going to hold hands with another guy (not that there's anything wrong with that). I knew that Kersch had pushed my hand away not only because he could, but because my holding his hand was not cool. Now I knew for sure he was in there. I was sure his mind was still whole.

That was all I needed.

Kersch has continued to progress; he finished the Heart and Sole walk in May. As I caught my breath after finishing the 10k, I turned to see him coming steadily to the finish of the 5k. I cheered with the crowd, and then approached him and said, "Way to go, Kersch. It's nice to see you, as always."

He looked at me with a thin smile. I wasn't sure he knew who I was. "I'm Roy's dad," I said.

He leaned toward me, rolling his eyes, slightly irritated. "I *know!*"

He really had been in there the whole time.

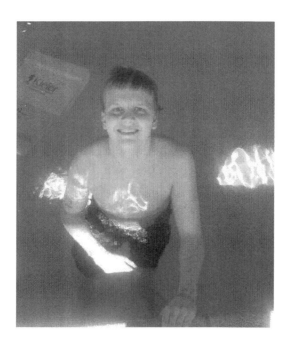

It's 2012 as I write this. The Iraq invasion and the Bush tax cuts have squandered a healthy budget surplus and plunged us into the Great Recession. It's not we, the "99%," who are dragging America down. We are the good guys.

Voices of millions of people are being raised against those forces bent on ripping our great country two, forces bent on creating division and anger as a means of mobilizing their voter base. Americans are seeing through the manipulation and propaganda.

President Obama brought us hope, change, and progress, in spite of an unprecedented level of Congressional obstruction. If you choose to do honest research, you can find a number of lists of his achievements online, and you can do your own fact checking.

Just a handful of successes for Americans:
- Overhauled the food safety system
- Passed the Hate Crimes bill
- Expanded access to medical care for everyone
- Invested in clean energy
- Overhauled the credit card industry; created The Consumer Financial Protection Bureau
- Eliminated Bin Laden and several other Al-Qaeda leaders
- Ended the Iraq invasion

Republicans actively opposed every single item on this list. Why, in 2012, did we vote them into office? They are the very folks who had screwed up the system in the first place.

Divided we fall, and it has been a divided society that has hurled the pendulum back and forth, in wide swings, in the last four elections. Our legislators have in turn chewed us up and passed us across the aisle to the next party with each swing.

We live in a society that's in shambles, where anger runs high, where hope runs low, and where there seems to be no relief in sight. As voters, as citizens, and as patriots, we can change that.

I hope that after reading this book, and recognizing the similarities between the state of the union now and the state of the union as it was in 2005, you'll consider voting in 2012, and voting for the right kind of change in Congress. I know it's crazy to hope that this would be the final time the pendulum swings. It's my hope that at least we will allow President Obama to finish the job of fixing America and the economy, and that we will restore a Democratic majority to Congress. I am confident that all of us, including the half of us 99% who are cynical about the Democrats, will benefit and become better off as a result.

Thank you for reading.

Made in the USA
Lexington, KY
13 July 2012